D0128675

Eco-Touring

This book is dedicated to our families, with whom we traveled on safari,
or from whom we are away at times.

A FIREFLY BOOK

This edition published in the United States in 1998

Copyright © 1993 by Streiffert Förlag AB, Stockholm

All rights reserved. No part of this work covered by the copyrights herein may be reproduced or used in any form or by any means—graphic, electronic or mechanical, including photocopying, recording, taping or information storage and retrieval systems—without the prior written permission of the publisher.

Cataloguing in Publication Data

Elander, Magnus, 1946–
Eco-touring : the ultimate guide

Includes bibliographical references and index.
ISBN 1-55209-184-8

1. Ecotourism. 2. Natural areas – Guidebooks.
I. Widstrand, Staffan. II. Title.

G155.A1E42   1997   910'.2'02   C97-930887-9

Firefly Books (U.S.) Inc.
P.O. Box 1338, Ellicot Station
Buffalo, New York 14205

Printed and bound in Italy

98 99 00 01 6 5 4 3 2 1

Scientific adviser: Ragnar Hall
Design: Bo Streiffert in collaboration with the Authors
Maps: Stig Söderlind
Jacket design: Jean Lightfoot Peters
Jacket photos: Christer Fredriksson (leopard), Staffan Widstrand (rhino).
English translation: Rosetta Translations, London
Reproduced by: Scannrepro AB and Proffsrepro, Västerås, Sweden

Eco-Touring
THE ULTIMATE GUIDE

MAGNUS ELANDER &
STAFFAN WIDSTRAND

A FIREFLY BOOK

Foreword

The well-known saying "Every traveler has a tale to tell" sprang to mind when I read *Eco-Touring: The Ultimate Guide*. These are truly fascinating stories that transport the reader to some of the most exciting wildlife places in the world. The authors' vivid accounts and fine photographs will instill in the reader an irresistible wanderlust and a desire to share in the experiences described. Moreover, they will provide many thought-provoking moments and exciting journeys in the mind for those readers unable to set out immediately on their own adventures.

It is not at all surprising that public demand for this book, our Panda Book of the Year 1994, has resulted in its now being reprinted in a completely updated and considerably expanded version. There are now 30 main nature destinations covered in detail and more than 130 locations in nearby areas that are briefly described.

Staffan Widstrand and Magnus Elander are committed nature-travel guides who take us on well-planned journeys to the best wildlife places in the world, where they treat plant and animal life with care and respect. For them, eco-tourism to wildlife places must be done in ways that are not detrimental to the environment.

Over the centuries, man has left many, deep footprints in nature. Deforestation, the growth of agriculture, the regulation of rivers and the draining of wetlands have all contributed to changing the face of our natural surroundings. Sometimes, nature has been able to recover from these ingresses, but more often the footprints have been so deep that they will never fade.

Today we see the need for leaving the lightest of footprints on our wild surroundings; coming generations will inherit the Earth we leave them. Recycling, the sparing use of our natural resources, and the careful preservation of our remaining wildernesses are now accepted concepts in the wildlife policies of most countries. Anyone thinking to exploit our natural resources must now consider the consequences to wildlife and the natural surroundings.

For the sake of our wildernesses and of the wildlife that inhabits them, it is vital that this trend continues to strengthen and flourish.

Safe journey!

Ulriksdal, Sweden, May 1997

Monika Stridsman
General Secretary
World Wildlife Fund WWF Sweden

Contents

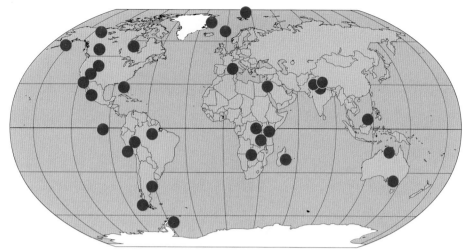

JAN PEDERSEN

The Teeming Bird Cliffs of the North Atlantic

The path from Goksøyr zig-zags up a treeless slope carpeted with grass and heather. We feel as if we are walking high in the Alps, but the distant roar of Atlantic breakers, and the tang of salt water and seaweed, remind us that Runde lies among the most seaward of the Norwegian "skerries"—tiny islands which are little more than rocks rearing up out of the sea. The heather moor levels off at the crown of the skerry. Ahead of us, a big, sturdy, dark-brown bird takes off and heads toward us with determined, threatening wingbeats. It is one of the great skuas that nest high on the islands and keep intruders away with aggressive, harassing dives. We stand firm and it changes tactics, landing a few yards from us. Now it pretends to be injured: first it behaves as if both its wings are broken, then it acts like one of its legs is injured. We have unwittingly entered the bird's private domain, close to its nest, so we walk on quickly.

After a while, the path disappears, leaving an almost vertical drop down to the sea, 650 feet (200 m) below us. The dizzying precipice is completely covered with puffins, guillemots, kittiwakes, gannets and fulmars.

Far below, the waves break with a dull sound against the dark rocks, and a cacophony from hundreds of thousands of birds is carried up the sloping cliff face by the rising air. With it comes the penetrating stench of their droppings. We rest for a moment to accustom our eyes and adjust our sense of balance to the height. With binoculars we can soon identify all the species in

Puffins on Herma Ness, Shetland (opposite page)

The puffin (below) is dependent on small fish such as herring, lesser sand eels, capelins and sprats for its survival. There is a clear relation between overfishing by man and the declining numbers of these birds.

STEFAN LUNDGREN

Half of the world's population of razorbills (above), about 250,000 pairs, breed on Látrabjarg, right out on the westernmost point of Iceland. They are also found in lesser numbers on nearly all the other North Atlantic bird cliffs.

The fulmar (left) is a decidedly pelagic bird. Related to the albatrosses, it is adapted to a life at sea. It often follows vessels, especially fishing boats, and comes ashore only to breed. This specimen was photographed in Herma Ness, Shetland.

the colony, but we'll have to scramble down to get close to them.

A little way down the slope we find tufts of thick grass to use as handholds. Puffins, with their big, red parrot bills, peer out from hollows between the overgrown rocks, and a great swarm of them circles as if waiting for some invisible air-traffic controller to give them clearance to land. Neat rows of fish line their beaks like silvery mustaches. Tens of thousands of pairs make their homes on a slope called Lundeura, just to the left of us.

Suddenly a herring gull joins in the proceedings. It selects a victim among the puffins and tries to force it to let go of its catch. Finally it grabs the puffin by the neck, there is a struggle, and the puffin drops its catch of lesser sand eels. The gull quickly releases the mugged bird and dives to scoop up its booty. But so do a whole flock of gulls who have been watching. We never see who got what. But most of the puffins bring their catches safely home to their young. When the chicks have been fed, some of the parents indulge in a brief glide on motionless wings. They may be inspired by the fulmars, those skilled fliers that breed highest up in the rookery.

At the foot of the slope, near the water, we climb past galleries of kittiwakes. Their nests are built very close together—tightly packed like a multistory Hong Kong tenement. No cliff ledge seems too small for them, and there must be a hundred thousand of these noisy tenants crowded into barely a mile of bird cliff. When one bird is disturbed, which happens regularly, this becomes a matter of urgent anxiety for all the rest. With an ear-splitting noise, they all fly up together. There's a serious disturbance when a white-tailed eagle sweeps around the Runde cliffs. For a few clamorous minutes, the cliff slope looks as if a giant has shaken out the contents of a feather pillow. When the birds have settled down again and the volume of their warning calls has diminished somewhat, we climb back up on all fours to begin the hike back to our base.

The impressive wingspan of the gannet (above) means that it often has trouble with its neighbors when taking off or landing.
Some 20,000 pairs of gannets nest close together (below) on Bass Rock, an island in the Firth of Forth, Scotland.

The shag (right) is found on many of the bird cliffs, but the colonies seldom consist of more than a few hundred pairs. The colony on the island of Runde, southern Norway, with almost 2,000 pairs, is deemed one of the biggest.

Description

• *Bjørnøya*, Svalbard, Norway:
The largest rookeries are located at the southern part of the island, where the coastal cliffs ascend steeply to 1,300 feet (400 m). Fulmars (50,000 pairs), guillemots (245,000 pairs), Brünnich's guillemots (105,000 pairs), little auks (10,000 pairs) and kittiwakes (100,000 pairs) nest here. Black guillemots, puffins, Arctic skuas and great skuas are also found here. During the autumn migration, the island is an important stop-over area for post-breeding barnacle geese from Svalbard.

• *Røst*, Norway:
The southernmost group of islands in the Lofoten archipelago, with Norway's largest colony of puffins (previously 700,000 pairs, but decreasing). There are also fulmars, storm petrels, Leach's petrels, shags, kittiwakes, razorbills, guillemots and black guillemots. Landing is prohibited on all islands except Vedøya during the breeding season. Ferry and air service from Bodø to Røstlandet. Easy-to-arrange boat trips to the neighboring bird islands. Youth hostel, private rooms (locally called "rorbucamping") and campsite.

• *Runde*, Norway:
Southernmost seabird rookery in Norway, housing puffins (75,000 pairs), kittiwakes (50,000 pairs) and guillemots (10,000 pairs). In addition, Europe's largest shag colony (2,000 pairs), gannets, great skuas and razorbills. The white-tailed eagle is common in the winter. Ferry from Torvik or by car from Ålesund (nearest city). A bridge connects Runde with the mainland. Daily boat trips to the bird cliffs. Hotel, campsite and food store.

• *Mykines* and *Mykineshólmur*, Faroe Islands:
Westernmost islands in the Faroe archipelago. Steep rocky coastline with grassy slopes harboring nesting fulmars (50,000 pairs), storm petrels (50,000 pairs), kittiwakes (20,000 pairs) and puffins (125,000 pairs). In addition, Manx shearwaters, Leach's storm petrels, gannets, shags, Arctic skuas, great skuas, guillemots, razorbills and black guillemots. Bus from Tórshavn to Sørvágur, and boat or helicopter service to Mykines.

• *Sandoy*, Faroe Islands:
Seabird colonies around most of the island. Fulmars (50,000 pairs), storm petrels (50,000 pairs), kittiwakes (20,000 pairs), guillemots (15,000 pairs) and puffins (70,000 pairs). Also, Manx shearwaters, shags, great skuas, razorbills and black guillemots.

• *Herma Ness*, Unst, Shetland Islands:
Peninsula covered by grassy moors, marshes and a rocky coast abounding with rookeries (a total of 70,000 pairs). A large colony of gannets (10,000 pairs) and puffins

(25,000 pairs). In addition, fulmars, shags, Arctic skuas, great skuas (600 pairs), kittiwakes, guillemots and razorbills.

• *St. Kilda*, Scotland:
Isolated group of islands west of the Outer Hebrides with one of the largest seabird colonies in the North Atlantic: nesting gannets (50,000 pairs), puffins (230,000 pairs), fulmars (60,000 pairs), storm petrels (10,000 pairs) and Leach's storm petrels (10,000 pairs). Also shags, great skuas, kittiwakes, guillemots, razorbills and black guillemots.

• *Rhum*, Scotland:
A large island with a rocky coastline and a mountainous interior. A mixture of marshes, grasslands and low shrubs. Houses one of the largest colonies of Manx shearwaters in the North Atlantic (100,000 pairs). Smaller numbers of fulmars, kittiwakes, guillemots, razorbills and puffins. Several pairs of golden eagles.

• *Forth Islands/Bass Rock*, Scotland:
A number of small islands in the Firth of Forth off the North Sea coast of Scotland, among others, the Isle of May and Bass Rock, with its large colony of gannets (21,000 pairs). Also guillemots (25,000 pairs), fulmars, cormorants, shags, kittiwakes, razorbills and puffins (15,000 pairs).

• *The Skelligs*, Ireland:
Tiny but sheer rocky islands off the southwest of Ireland with

gannets (22,000 pairs on Little Skellig) and storm petrels (10,000 pairs). In addition, fulmars, Manx shearwaters, kittiwakes, guillemots, razorbills and puffins.

• *Grímsey*, Iceland:
Island north of the mainland, on the Arctic Circle, with huge colonies of mainly kittiwakes and auks (100,000 pairs). The southernmost breeding place for little auks (1–2 pairs). Boat or air service from Akureyri.

• *Látrabjarg*, Iceland:
An immense rookery, located on the westernmost promontory of Iceland, with more than 1 million nesting birds, making it the largest seabird colony in the North Atlantic (excluding the little-auk colonies in East Greenland). Here there are more than 100,000 pairs of fulmars, the most numerous colony of razorbills in the world (250,000 pairs—50 percent of the world population), guillemots (400,000 pairs), puffins (100,000 pairs) and kittiwakes (50,000 pairs). Also shags and black guillemots. Bus or air service from Reykjavik to Stykkishólmur on Snæfellsnes. Ferry across Breidafjördur to Brjánslaekur, and then road connection.

• *Hælavíkurbjarg* and *Hornbjarg*, Iceland:
These two sanctuaries in the far northwest house altogether 1 million pairs of nesting kittiwakes, guillemots, Brünnich's guillemots and razorbills. Domestic air to Isafjördur and onwards by boat.

• *Scoresbysund*, Greenland:
At the mouth of the Scoresbysund fjord, strong tidal currents ensure ice-free water most of the year. These nutrient-rich waters feed the world's most numerous colonies of little auks. Around Kap Brewster, on the southern coast of the fjord, there are between 1 and 5 million nesting pairs, and on the islands and on Liverpool Land north of the fjord, another 1 to 5 million pairs breed. Also, Brünnich's guillemot (30,000 pairs) and fulmars, kittiwakes and black guillemots.

One of a pair of great skuas takes off from its nest to chase away an intruder.

Pink Birds among White Horses
Parc Naturel Régional de Camargue, France

"The best way to experience La Camargue is on horseback!," Richard Llop firmly maintains over a glass of *pastis* in the bar of the little *pension* at Les Arnelles. He is one of the *gardians*, the local cowboys of the region, and has ridden and worked with horses and bulls since his childhood. He rides as if the horse were part of him—or vice versa.

"On horseback you can get about easily, regardless of roads or trails, through mud and water, quick or slow, and you can take a good deal of kit with you—good food and drink, for example," he adds with a twinkle in his eye.

"Apart from this, you must be on horseback to get into the actual reserve. Cars and walkers are not allowed," adds his colleague Jean-Pierre.

"The animals and birds aren't afraid of horses in the way they are of people and cars, so you can get much closer to the flamingos, herons and other birds. The horses roam freely in the delta all year round, you see, and have done so for centuries. They and the birds know one another, they're old friends. *Bien sûr!*"

Siesta in the shade of a pair of dense umbrella pines, and all around us stretches one of southern Europe's last large and relatively undisturbed nature areas: mile upon mile with sand dunes, umbrella-pine groves, freshwater marshes, salt lakes, reed beds, streams, tributary rivers, dried-up mud flats, and tamarisk thickets. The air is filled with the mating calls or the alarm cries of shorebirds: the sad sound of the avocet and the redshank's endless piping, the stuttering lament of the black-winged stilt and, at a distance, the

CHRESTER FREDRIKSSON

STAFFAN WIDSTRAND

The flamingos (left) breed in the shallow salt lakes of the Camargue. During the day, they spread out in loose flocks over the delta area to feed. Mornings and evenings, they are often seen flying between their feeding grounds and the lakes where they breed (previous page).

Richard Llop (below) is a gardian who, to a great extent, has grown up in the saddle on the white horses, out in the Rhône delta. In the summer he earns his living by showing visitors around the delta on horseback.

dry, gooselike cackle of greater flamingos, "les flamants," as they are called hereabouts. High above, a flock of multicolored bee-eaters whirls about after insects, while the wind is heavy with the spicy scents of thyme, oregano, sage and rosemary.

As the sun goes down, the colors turn a warmer reddish-yellow, the shadows lengthen. The landscape shows up with greater clarity, and the birds seem to become livelier again. This is the flamingos' favorite time for flying. Restlessness spreads like wildfire among them and they simply have to be up and flying. From their feeding grounds all over the delta, they are now bound for their safe night roosts either deep in the reserve or somewhere in the wide saltpans.

A long skein of the gaudy birds comes in low over a group of mounted birdwatchers. For these unwonted riders, turning around in the saddle and holding on to the reins, while at the same time looking through their binoculars at the birds in flight, is not without its complications …

STAFFAN WIDSTRAND

Description

La Camargue is the vast, waterlogged delta land, where the river Rhône at first divides into two and later reaches the Mediterranean. The landscape here is a mixture of dry steppes, marshes, saltpans, paddyfields, fresh- or saltwater lakes, pastures and farming lands. The farming areas are also rich in birdlife, as are the saltpans in the southeast (Étang de Fangassier especially). The latter is the main breeding area for the greater flamingo, and is probably the best area in the Camargue to see larger flocks of these pink birds. Best at dawn or dusk. These saltpans are the largest in all Europe. The paddyfields are home to many interesting birds, especially after harvest. A large heronry (night herons and little egrets) is found at Mas de l'Abbé, northeast of the town Aigues-Mortes.

Camargue is a piece of nature living at man's mercy, squeezed between the sea, the oil refineries of Marseille, the intense farming areas, the motorways and the deluxe vacation marinas of the Languedoc coast. It is considered one of the most important bird areas of Europe.

In the central part, around Étang de Vaccarès, is the most protected area, Réserve Nationale de Camargue, created in 1972 with the help of the WWF. Outside this are other areas with varying levels of protection, all part of the Parc Naturel Régional de Camargue. The area to the west of the park itself, La Petite Camargue, has a rich birdlife and also a certain level of protection.

The delta is still used for grazing traditional black cattle—a small and ancient breed—under semi-wild conditions. The famous white horses of the Camargue are also of a breed of their own—strong, short-legged and easy to ride—bred, since the days of antiquity, for surviving life in the marshes. It is one of the oldest horse breeds in Europe, and the horses are still used for tending the cattle of the delta.

Camargue is an important wintering site for ducks (250,000–400,000) from all over Europe.

Fauna of interest

MAMMALS: Wild boar, nutria (introduced), otter, small spotted genet, stone marten, red fox, stoat/ermine.

BIRDS: Greater flamingo (6,000–13,000 pairs), roller, bee-eater, hoopoe, eight species of heron, white stork, red-headed pochard, Egyptian vulture, booted eagle, short-toed eagle, black kite, peregrine falcon, lesser kestrel, gull-billed tern, whiskered tern, slender-billed gull, pratincole, little bittern, great spotted cuckoo, barn owl, little owl, scops owl and hundreds of thousands of wintering ducks.

REPTILES: European pond terrapin, Hermann's tortoise.

Seasons

Spring comes sunny but cool, owing to the eternal wind—Le Mistral—coming down

through the whole valley of the Rhône, sometimes even into mid-May. Summer is between June and September, with lots of sun and high temperatures. Winters are usually mild.

The most protected areas are forbidden to visitors, except those on horseback, who are permitted to enter out of the breeding season.

How to get there

International or domestic flights to Marseille, or domestic flight to Nîmes, and bus/rented car from there. Or train to Arles and bus/rented car from there.

Accommodation/food/camping

Almost all lodging available is gathered around the village Saintes-Maries-de-la-Mer, or along the road leading there from Arles. Guest ranches, hotels and family *pensions* abound. *Pensions* also in Le Sambuc and Salin-de-Giraud. Camping allowed only in two sites in Saintes. Getting around is best on horseback. Moving by jeep, car, bicycle or on foot is also possible, but then you are restricted to the few roads. Most birds and mammals can in fact be seen from the roads. All means of transport can be rented in Saintes. Jeep tours and horse rides are operated daily.

Other areas

Parco Nazionale del Gran Paradiso, Italy. Has probably the highest density of mammals of any alpine area in Europe. Comprises 225 square miles (585 sq km) of alpine meadows, forests and eternal snow. Highest peak, Gran Paradiso, reaches 13,320 feet (4061 m). Ibex (3,500), Alpine chamois (6,000–7,000), Alpine marmot, golden eagle, eagle owl, red-billed chough, Alpine chough, wallcreeper, white-winged snow finch. Good hiking trails and lodging. Camping permitted.

The Danube Delta, Romania. Comprises 1,160 square miles (3000 sq km) of reed beds, with a labyrinth of lakes, islands, rivers and channels. Species like in the Camargue, and also white pelican, Dalmatian pelican, glossy ibis, little cormorant, all species of heron in Europe, white-tailed eagle, lesser spotted eagle, red-footed falcon, saker falcon, black stork. National-park status will soon be conferred.

Villages Murighol and Crisan are good starting points. Local fishermen arrange boat trips. Wintering site for 1.5 million ducks and geese, among these a major part of the world population of red-breasted geese.

The Volga Delta, Russia. Comprises 2,470 square miles (6400 sq km) of marshes, lakes and reed beds where the river Volga reaches the Caspian Sea. Here lies a reserve called Astrakhan Zapovednik. Species like in the Danube delta, but in far greater numbers. As well, 5–7 million ducks and geese winter or pass by during spring or autumn migration.

Biebrza, Poland. Comprises 500 square miles (800 sq km) of wet forests, bogs, reed beds, lakes and riverine grazing land, close to the border of Byelorussia. One of the few large wetlands in Europe that is still grazed in the ancient way. White-tailed eagle, lesser spotted eagle, greater spotted eagle, short-toed eagle, roller, whiskered tern, white stork, black stork, woodpeckers, corn crake, aquatic warbler, beaver, otter.

Parque Nacional de Doñana, Spain. A 190-square-mile (500-sq-km) national park and a 97-square-mile (250-sq-km) buffer zone in the inland delta of the river Guadalquivir, on the Atlantic coast. Sand dunes and forests of umbrella pines along the coast. Inland lies Las Marismas, with its periodic saline and fresh-water lakes and marshes, dry steppes and great cork oaks. Rich in wildlife also outside the reserves. Most African habitat in Europe. Species like in the Camargue, plus red deer, fallow deer, Spanish lynx, Egyptian mongoose, griffon vulture, black vulture, Spanish imperial eagle (15 pairs), marbled duck, white-headed duck, purple gallinule, black stork, sand grouse, azure-winged magpie. Also 10,000–20,000 flamingos, 80,000 graylag geese and 200,000 ducks winter here. 350 species of bird seen. Lodging in El Rocío and Matalascanas.

During the twentieth century, the cattle egret has spread out from Africa over large parts of the world, including the Camargue.

MAGNUS ELANDER

Among Arctic Muskoxen and Arctic Wolves
The National Park in North and East Greenland

By mid-June, winter at last begins to loosen its grip on the coastal tundra north of latitude 73. The temperature stays above freezing twenty-four hours a day, and the snow cover shrinks noticeably day by day. The water level rises, and many small lakes and tarns overflow their banks. The surface layer of the surrounding permafrosted ground thaws out and the low-lying areas become almost impassable. Swarms of newly hatched midges hum in the air, and here and there snow buntings let their melancholy song be heard. Rust-red knots fill the upper air with their curlewlike calls, while sanderlings flutter low over the ground on vibrating wings, performing their monotonous aerial display.

Red-throated divers and king eiders make daily reconnaissance flights over their intended breeding lakes, to be able to establish themselves as soon as the ice breaks up. While the tops of the 3,200-foot (1000-m) coastal mountains are still sheathed in sparkling winter snow, the animal life of the High Arctic revives for the few weeks of summer.

Ten muskoxen graze lazily in loose formation on the southern slope at the foot of one of the mountains. A single calf—this year's—frisks about in the warm sunshine, with its mother reassuringly close. The idyll seems complete. But two light-colored Arctic wolves are slowly approaching along the shore of the still-frozen sea. The larger of the two is a dirty yellowish-white and in the process of changing to its summer fur, while the small one is all white, with its winter fur obviously intact. First they prowl round our lookout position high up on the roof of a long-abandoned trapping station. It is highly probable that they have never been close to human habitation before; they do not seem greatly impressed, but soon continue at a steady trot across the sodden ground. They have caught sight of the muskoxen!

The muskoxen have no inkling yet of the danger. In the half-century since the wolf was eradicated from the national-park area, they have grown accustomed to living without their archenemy. These muskoxen are not as alert as their ancestors must once have been. They are certainly not as watchful as they ought to be now that the Arctic wolf is recolonizing its former territory.

Silently the wolves get closer, alternately walking and trotting. They head for the cow with the calf. The large male wolf is now so close that he can actually sniff the rear quarters of one of the musk-oxen without being detected. Too late, the cow and her calf realize what is happening. The calf hurries to its mother's hindquarters and tries to make itself as invisible as possible. But two pairs of wolf eyes see it all.

Normally muskoxen would instantly arrange themselves for collective defense. The attacking wolves, however, have already preempted any chance of the oxen grouping themselves in their

traditional semi-circular defensive formation. Instead they flee in panic—it is each for himself! The cow and her calf are left behind, and the wolves invite them to a dance of death. One of them makes continuous mock attacks on the cow, while the other one goes for the calf. The cow fights desperately, trying to repel the attackers with her sharp horns, but after just a few minutes she has to give up. She

The white Arctic wolf (opposite page) has migrated back into East Greenland from the center of its range in northern Canada, a distance of more than 1,200 miles (2000 km). After a long, cold winter, with shortage of food for the wolves, the late, bright spring arrives with newborn muskox calves as welcome prey. When wolves attack, the muskoxen form a living defensive wall, with the season's calves to the rear (right). Nevertheless, the oxen find it hard to defend themselves, and the wolves make short work of one of the calves. This is one of the first occasions that the hunt has been documented in photographs.

is unable to defend her calf any longer and gallops wildly after the other adult animals. The calf stays, deserted and left to its executioners. The wolves bring down the calf and finish it off with fatal bites to throat and belly.

All around, life goes on as if the drama had never taken place. From its position high up on a boulder, a snowy owl keeps watch over its domain. That the boulder is a favorite perch is shown by the pretty, orange-colored lichens that thrive on the nutritious owl droppings, amply replenished over many years. With their glowing colors, the lichens are visible a long way off among the otherwise muted hues of the landscape.

This part of North and East Greenland was designated a national park in 1974 to protect a unique and sensitive High Arctic region from uncontrolled hunting and from the exploitation of any oil or minerals there. History has shown that small changes in the environment can be disastrous for animals that already live on the very margins of what is possible. Implicit in the national-park idea is not only the preservation of the animals in their natural environments, but also the protection of their migratory routes. The Arctic wolf, which people once actively eradicated from Greenland, migrated back from Canada in the 1980s, a sign of how right this objective is.

More than a million little auks breed at Kap Brewster and the Volquart Boon coast, at the mouth of Scoresbysund Fjord (right). The water remains ice-free for a large part of the year around the mouth of this fjord, and seals, whales and birds of various kinds gather here. Great flocks of king eiders (below) often rest here during migration.

Arctic hares (above) live all year round on the tundra and the lower mountain slopes, whereas the red-throated diver (below) is just a summer visitor during the short time when tundra pools are free of ice.

ANDERS GEIDEMARK

Description

Greenland, the world's largest island, belongs geographically to the North American continent. Politically, however, it is a self-governing part of Denmark. The national park in North and East Greenland covers 355,240 square miles (920 000 sq km) and is at present by far the largest in the world, being more than twice the size of Sweden. The entire national park lies north of the Arctic Circle and is mostly covered by inland ice. A treeless landscape dissected by fjords extends along the coast, and ranges from desertlike plains to alpine areas with peaks close to 9,850 feet (3000 m).

At the mouth of the Scoresbysund fjord, just south of the national park's border, the water is kept ice-free all year round by the currents and the tide—an oasis for animal life in the otherwise frozen sea. Auks in their hundreds of thousands come here to forage from the breeding colonies at Kap Brewster, Raffles Ø and Kap Höegh. Ringed seals are common all year round, and during the short summer bearded seals and walruses are seen regularly, and sometimes even narwhals and minke whales. The area is good polar bear territory.

Local hunters are active at all seasons and often possess the best knowledge of where and when to see the animals. Farther into the fjord is Jameson Land, with terrestrial tundra-living animals like muskoxen, Arctic foxes and, with some luck, an Arctic wolf. Bird-fauna is rich in nesting Arctic waders, but above all also in moulting geese. Some 11,000 pink-footed geese and 3,000 barnacle geese congregate here in the late summer.

Farther north is breeding territory for several High Arctic birds such as the king eider, ivory gull, various waders and long-tailed skua. Muskoxen are typical, Arctic foxes are common and the Arctic wolf has bred several times during the past decade. Seals abound along the coast, and walruses show up regularly. The drift ice in Foster Bugt is the haunt of polar bears.

Fauna of interest

BIRDS: Greenland falcon, red-throated diver, great northern diver, fulmar, pink-footed goose, barnacle goose, Brent goose, king eider, long-tailed duck, ptarmigan, some ten species of waders (e.g., knot, sanderling, gray phalarope), Arctic skua, long-tailed skua, glaucous gull, Arctic tern, ivory gull, Brünnich's guillemot, little auk, black guillemot, snowy owl, raven, snow bunting.

MAMMALS: Arctic wolf, polar bear, muskox, walrus, Arctic hare, Arctic fox, stoat, ringed seal, bearded seal, hooded seal, harp seal, narwhal, minke whale.

Seasons

Most birds arrive at the end of May (colony-breeding pelagic birds somewhat earlier) and

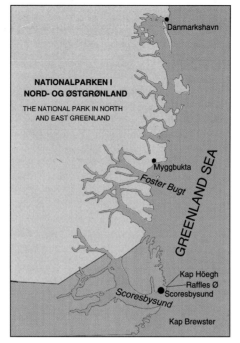

stay until August. Most rewarding time for birds is in June, but fjords are not ice-free and open for boat transportation until mid-July. Late summer is for practical reasons the easiest time to visit the area, and also the best season for seals and whales. The climate is High Arctic, meaning long, cold winters and short, chilly summers. The average temperature for July does not exceed 40°F (5°C) and winter temperatures between -22 and –58°F (–30° and –50°C) are not uncommon. Midnight sun prevails from mid-May until mid-August in the southern part of the park, and even longer in the far north.

How to get there

Air service from Iceland to Scoresbysund. From here one has to charter private transport by boat or dogsled to the bird rookeries on the outer coast or to the tundra. Two- and three-week expeditions are available annually to various places within the southernmost parts of the national park, and access is then often by chartered plane from Akureyri on Iceland. Cruises featuring small-craft side-trips into the network of fjords are sometimes organized and offer excellent opportunities to encounter wildlife in the pack-ice as well as ashore. Traveling privately on your own requires permission from the Danish Polar Centre in Copenhagen. Off-road vehicles are not allowed.

Accommodation/food/camping

There is no resident population north of Scoresbysund. This is also the location of the area's only general store. Visitors are advised to bring all necessary provisions from Iceland. No accommodation in the national park. Camping is permitted in most places in the park as long as instructions from authorities

regarding personal safety, littering and wildlife are obeyed. Previous experience hiking in the wilderness is mandatory when traveling on your own.

Other areas

Søndre Strømfjord, southwestern Greenland, offers a good view over the inland ice and is the most accessible place to watch muskoxen. The population here exceeds 3,000 animals, and they may frequently be spotted close to the airport. In addition, caribou and Greenland falcon are often seen.

Ellesmere Island National Park Reserve, Northwest Territories, Canada, was established in 1988 and covers 14,600 square miles (37,800 sq km). The park reserve is a High Arctic desert, receiving annual precipitation of only 2.4 inches (60 mm). In addition to mountains and glaciers, there is Lake Hazen, one of the largest lakes north of the Arctic Circle. Interesting animals are the muskox, caribou, Arctic hare, Arctic wolf, Arctic fox and some 30 species of birds. Polar bears are uncommon but occasionally seen along the coast.

Bathurst Island "Polar Bear Pass", Northwest Territories, Canada. A wide, level valley about 19 miles (30 km) long, running across the island, with, by High Arctic standards, remarkably abundant wildlife. Muskox, Arctic fox and Arctic hare abound. Breeders include Brent goose, snow goose, king eider, gray plover and snowy owl.

Ust'Lensky Zapovednik, Yakutia, Russia. With its more than 38,600 square miles (100,000 sq km) the largest nature reserve in Eurasia. Includes half of the Lena River delta. Breeding place for Ross's gull, Steller's eider, Brent goose and a wide variety of shorebirds. The reserve also includes the New Siberian Islands and a major share of the Laptev Sea, with polar bear, wolf, walrus, beluga and narwhal. A good starting point for visitors is the Lena-Nordenskiold scientific station, 62 miles (100 km) northwest of Tiksi.

Snowy owl appear here only in a good year for lemmings, when they rear large broods.

STEFAN LUNDGREN

Polar Bears and Walruses
Svalbard, Norway

To port lies the vast Atlantic, to starboard Spitsbergen itself: a rugged landscape of snow-clad massifs, mountain peaks and glaciers. And, of course, the midnight sun. Only when banks of evening mist drift by is reality obscured for a while, giving the eyes a moment's rest.

We turn in late, but cannot sleep. We are right in the middle of the ice. It groans and screeches, and the whole vessel shudders as it thuds into the ice floes. A former sealer, the MV *Polarstar* shakes and vibrates with the climbing engine revs as the captain tries to butt the floes aside. Cutting a way through them is now out of the question. This is not crumbly fjord ice, but thick, multiyear polar ice, blown here by the last few days' north wind from the Arctic Ocean. The ice is, however, welcome—not perhaps for those trying to sleep, and

definitely not for the helmsman, but welcome because it signals the start of our genuine Arctic experience. The ice means seals and bears.

Small flocks of little auks and Brünnich's guillemots constantly wing ahead of the ship. Solitary bearded seals drift by on the floes, and two fulmars soar to stern, but there is no big game in sight as yet.

Through his binoculars, the skipper examines every ice floe in the dazzling sunlight. We cross latitude 80 degrees N, and the few remaining on deck are rewarded with the sight of an off-white ivory gull. Only its black feet, and dark beak and eyes, reveal its presence. The rest is lost in the white glare.

"Walrus, walrus!" In response to the call, the helmsman alters course and heads slowly for three dark lumps on a far-off ice floe. The vessel chugs cautiously nearer. The walruses become bigger and more imposing. They seem to have no desire at all to plunge into the ice-cold water. Their long tusks gleam yellowish-white, and their whiskers are as thick as lead pencils. Walrus tusks are the ivory of the North and were a desirable commodity as far back as Viking times. They look at us suspiciously and seem to be considering slipping into the water, but nothing happens. A single walrus breaks the surface in front of the three, and with a snort it blows, almost like a whale, to ventilate its lungs. Its back, visible above the water, and its disproportionately small head give it an easily recognizable profile. A deep breath, a powerful arching of its back, and it dives without a sound. The last image remaining on the retina is of its hind flippers, perfectly parallel, and tarsals stretched.

Our journey continues eastward, and the landscape becomes flatter and more barren as we come closer to Kong Karls Land. At last someone spots what we have all been looking for these last few days: a polar bear! At

All year round, the polar bear's habitat is the drift-ice (opposite page), where it hunts for seals. Strange smells can make it very curious (right), and it is notorious for breaking into houses and huts where it thinks it can find something edible.

In winter, when the sea near the coast is frozen, walruses move farther out to the open water. They eat mostly mussels, and only exceptionally kill seals (below).

MAGNUS ELANDER

that distance it looks like a dirty-yellow blob on the crispy, blue-white mass of ice. It is still far off, but the ice does not let us get any closer. The bear pads along at right angles to our vessel's course. At last the captain finds the weak point in the ice floe that was blocking our progress and splits it in the middle: full speed ahead! The bear gets up on its hind legs to listen and to take in the strange smells. With a gigantic leap, it jumps onto another ice floe. Carefully we glide quite close, with the engine just ticking over. The bear's coat looks whiter now, but by no means snowy white. With its snout in the air, the bear wags its head from side to side, then

The little auk (above) is one of the world's most numerous bird species. A quarter of a million pairs breed around Ingeborgsfjell, near Bellsund. In total there are more than a million pairs on Svalbard—despite the fact that many parts of it look as bleak and inhospitable as Leifdefjord (below).

lumbers away from us with a gait that combines lithe power with sullen clumsiness. When the distance between drifting ice floes is too great, it plunges head-first into the water. A tremendous splash, a few strokes, and then, with the help of its claws, it is up on the next piece of ice. The polar bear, the lonely wanderer of the Arctic.

MATS FORSBERG

Description

Svalbard, 620 miles (1000 km) north of the Arctic Circle, is a group of islands that includes five larger (the largest is Spitsbergen) and many smaller islands. The landscape is Alpine, with peaks between 3,280 and 3,900 feet (1000 and 1200 m) and a few even up to 5,580 feet (1700 m). More than 50 percent of the area is covered by glaciers, many active and calving into the sea. In the far north there is midnight sun for four and a half months, while the sun never rises during the correspondingly long polar night. The Gulf Stream brings relatively warm water to the west coast of Spitsbergen, making it mostly ice-free. The summer is short, with an average temperature of between 32 and 50°F (0 and 10°C). The eastern part of Svalbard receives most of the snow and also has the shortest season with no snow on the ground. The waters to the east are permanently filled with drift-ice from the Arctic Ocean. In 1973, 3 national parks and 15 bird sanctuaries were established, covering 55 percent of the total area of the islands.

Sørspitsbergens National Park, 1,804 square miles (4673 sq km), includes the southern parts of Spitsbergen. Hornsund, one of the most spectacular fjords, houses a giant colony of hundreds of thousands of breeding little auks. The Sophia and Lucia ridges have mixed colonies, with Brünnich's guillemot and kittiwake in the precipitous cliffs. In the inner parts of the fjord, the ice cover is still unbroken in June, leaving safe sun-bathing places for ringed seals and a good chance to spot a polar bear. On the tundra, barnacle geese and Arctic skuas nest. Chamberlain Valley in Bellsund has tundra, with caribou and grazing geese, both barnacle and Brent. In the drift-ice on the eastern side, thousands of harp seals molt, and at Sandhamna, near Sørkapp, there is a good chance of spotting killer whales and other species of whales.

Prins Karls Forland National Park, 247 square miles (640 sq km), a long and narrow island off the west coast of Spitsbergen covered with a mixture of coastal plains, high mountain peaks and numerous minor glaciers. Large colonies of nesting common eiders and all three species of geese occurring on Svalbard. The island is surrounded by an extension of the warm Gulf Stream, and the national park is the site of the northernmost nesting rookeries for guillemots in the world, as well as the northernmost population of harbor seals.

Nordvest-Spitsbergen National Park, 1,268 square miles (3283 sq km), covers the northwestern corner of Spitsbergen and a number of smaller islands. Ytre Norskøya and the island Fuglesangen house nesting colonies of little auks, black guillemots, puffins and Brünnich's guillemots. Reindyrsflya, the most extensive tundra area on Spitsbergen, is breeding territory for various waders, king eiders and red-throated divers. Caribou and Arctic fox are common sights here. The small island of Moffen is the haunt of a growing population of walruses. Danskøya, where Andrée a century ago started his doomed balloon flight toward the North Pole, is now a

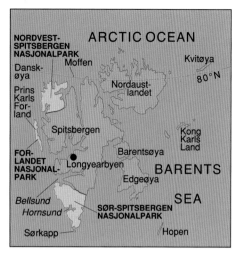

breeding place for thousands of little auks.

Nordaust-Svalbard Wildlife Reserve, 7,348 square miles (19 030 sq km), is the most extensive protected area covering Nordaustlandet, parts of northeastern Spitsbergen, Kvitøya and Kong Karls Land. The last is the most important area for polar bears in this part of the Arctic.

Søraust-Svalbard Wildlife Reserve, 2,490 square miles (6 450 sq km), covers the two large islands, Edgeøya and Barentsøya, as well as a number of smaller islands. It is inhabited by some 1,500–2,000 caribou, and the polar bear is common, particularly in the winter. Numerous breeding places for pink-footed and Brent geese. At Diskobukta, on Edgeøya, there is a major colony of kittiwakes attracting both Arctic foxes and polar bears. Ivory gulls are always present in the drift-ice. At Andrée-tangen, the walruses give birth to their calves.

Fauna of interest

BIRDS: Five species of auks, pink-footed goose, barnacle goose, Brent goose, king eider, gray phalarope, other waders, three species of skuas, ivory gull, Sabine's gull.

MAMMALS: Polar bear, caribou, Arctic fox, walrus, five species of seal, minke whale, beluga.

Seasons

Only from mid-June to mid-September. Nature blooms during the short summer while, the rest of the year, harsh winterlike conditions prevail. The west coast of Spits-

bergen is ice-free all year round, but the fjords are icebound and not accessible for normal cruise ships. Eastern Svalbard is always more difficult to reach because of the heavy drift-ice.

How to get there

Air service from Tromsö, in northern Norway, to Longyearbyen. Most tourist expeditions and round trips by boat start from here and cover various parts of Svalbard. Hiking along the coast and in the mountains can be rewarding, but to encounter walruses and polar bears, the best choice is a cruise boat. Trips on your own are possible, but you have to be completely self-supporting. Ask local authorities (the so-called Sysselmannen) in Longyearbyen for regulations and how to get there.

Accommodation/food/camping

One hotel and guestrooms in Longyearbyen and a hostel in Barentsburg and Pyramiden. Cabins and huts, private and state-owned, all over Svalbard, may not be used by tourists for overnighting. Camping outside residential areas is possible with the permission of the Sysselmannen, who also gives information about necessary safety equipment and required insurance. Restaurants, café and kiosk in Longyearbyen, as well as a general store with a limited selection.

Other areas

Taymyr Peninsula, Russia, covering 154,450 square miles (400 000 sq km), is almost as large as Sweden, and includes Eurasia's most extensive tundra. Important breeding places for the red-breasted goose, Brent goose, knot and gray plover. Home to the world's largest population of caribou. Arctic foxes abound, and the coasts along the Kara Sea and the Laptev Sea have polar bears, ringed seals, walruses and belugas. Nearest major city is Norilsk.

Wrangel Island, Russia, in the Arctic Ocean between the Chukchi Sea and the East Siberian Sea, is surrounded by ice most of the year. Polar bears are common. Summer feeding among thousands of walruses on the beaches around Cape Blossom, the southwestern promontory. In addition, several species of seals, gray whales and millions of auks. Trips start from Nome, Alaska.

The best chance of seeing a polar bear is on the drift-ice off eastern Svalbard.

MAGNUS ELANDER

A Million Birds of Prey
Elat, Israel

Approaching from the southwest, several hundred buzzards glide in a seemingly never-ending formation low over the crest of Mount Yoash. They glide on stiff wings, now and then interrupted by a few wingbeats. The chill of night still hangs over the mountains, but since the first hour of light the heat of the desert sun has been creating the conditions necessary to cause thermals—rising currents of warm air—which mean efficient flight economy for avian gliders A flock of buzzards begins to soar to test the lifting capacity of the thermals. The loose formation tightens up into a great gyre, and at a distance the circling raptors are reminiscent of swarming midges. Within a short while the birds encounter one of the invisible "hot-air lifts" and they begin to gain altitude, seemingly without exertion. Before long, they are out of sight of the naked eye. Along the

shores of the Gulf of Aqabah, the next wave of large raptors (birds of prey) is already on its way from the Sinai peninsula, and behind them yet another.

At half past eight, the first steppe eagles start to test whether the thermals are sufficiently strong to carry the largest and most powerful of these avian gliders. With heavy wingbeats one of the eagles takes off and circles low over the ground several times, but it fails to get enough support from the upward current. Within a few minutes it lands again on the barren mountainside, leaving the heat of the sun to work for another while. The lighter steppe buzzards, however, pass by in uninterrupted thousands, sometimes in the company of black kites, and now and then a solitary booted eagle. Later in the morning, the steppe eagles make another attempt. Starting in wide circles low over the ground, they are drawn into the upward gyres of buzzards, and then climb slowly aloft, higher and higher. With their huge wing span and powerfully splayed pinions, they mingle with the distinctly smaller buzzards in the aerial roundabout. A dozen black storks join in with the birds of prey to compete at gliding. As if at a given signal, the gyre dissolves and all the birds glide away on motionless wings, in a long necklace, to the north and northeast. They will cover a good distance before they slowly lose altitude and it is time to find a new thermal.

The lookout position on Mount Yoash, outside Elat, lies right under the busiest of the raptors' narrow flight corridors between their winter quarters in Africa and their breeding areas in Europe and Asia. Busloads of interested spectators from several countries stand here for days on end, gazing skywards to follow the soundless traffic overhead. The silence is broken only by discussions about what species a hard-to-identify eagle might belong to, or by an enthusiastic outburst when an unexpected silhouette turns up in the steady

An Egyptian vulture (opposite page) gliding low over the Negev desert. It is one of the many birds of prey that fly over this vast, barren desert region (below). The steppe buzzard (right) can seem big in its solitary majesty, but alongside a steppe eagle displaying its broad wingspan (above right), it looks small. Both are on their way to the Central Asian steppes.

stream of birds of prey: sometimes an Egyptian vulture, sometimes a spotted eagle. For hour after hour, hundreds, thousands, tens of thousands, representing at least a dozen species, fly over. The birds fly on without interruption until the heat of the day fades and the disc of the sun sinks into the Sinai desert. As the thermals diminish in strength, the birds lose altitude, and the precondition for their long-range, low-energy flight is gone for the day. In the twilight, eagles, buzzards and kites positively rain down from the skies. They quickly find themselves a spot to sleep on the stony, barren slopes of the desert hills or on the steep cliffs that rise from the dried-up watercourses. By the time darkness falls, the birds of prey have come to roost, sitting in scattered formations like darker spots in the ochre-colored stone rubble. Twelve hours' rest await them after twelve hours in the air. Just so long as their rest is not disturbed by prowling wolves, desert foxes or some solitary leopard.

The Bonelli's eagle (above) and the ibex (right) are characteristic species of the desert uplands around Elat, and can be seen all year round. Bonelli's eagle specializes in hunting desert partridges. The ibex feeds on the sparse vegetation around waterholes and dried-up riverbeds, or wadis, as they are called.

Description

Desert surrounds Elat, which lies at the head of the Gulf of Aqabah, the northern arm of the Red Sea, separating Sinai from the Arabian peninsula. At Elat, Israel's southern-most city, the land is squeezed to a narrow wedge between Egypt and Jordan. The city is circled by mountains. To the west and north are the Elat Mountains and the high plateaux of the southern Negev, reaching altitudes of 2,625 feet (800 m) above sea level, to the east the Mountains of Edom, with peaks of about 4,921 feet (1500 m). The mountains are heavily eroded, and the landscape is sculpted by sand, gravel, stones and loose rocks. Vegetation is scanty, and the colors of the naked ground reflect the underlying marine sedimentary rocks. Erratic rainfall and gravity carry the products of erosion down to the low-lying areas in the Arava Valley through a network of dry watercourses, or wadis, and ravines that cut into the mountain slopes. Wadis often support stands of low acacias, forming a sparse savannah-like forest in the ochre-colored environment. Occasionally, where the groundwater is close to the surface, there are small stands of date palms and doum palms. The Arava Valley extends 124 miles (200 km) north to the Dead Sea, a salt lake with no outlets, 1,293 feet (394 m) below sea level. The mountains along the lake ascend steeply and create several excellent vista points, such as Masada, Ein Gedi and Mezoke Dragot. The main attraction in Elat, besides the easily accessible coral reefs, is the migrating birds. Due to its strategic location as a land-bridge between Africa and Asia, masses of migrating birds pass here on their way between wintering areas in Africa and breeding grounds in Europe and western Asia. This is particularly true of the diurnal raptors. They take advantage of the thermals, formed as the sun heats up the ground, to move great distances with as little energy as possible. During spring migration, when there is a general move northeast, their reluctance to cross over open sea takes the raptors northwards along the western shore of the Red Sea, and they cross only when the sea narrows at the entrance to the Gulf of Suez. The next leading line is the shores of the Gulf of Aqabah, which takes them straight over Elat. Annually between 500,000 and 1,200,000 (!) raptors, representing some 30 different species, pass through. Top counts during spring migration (February to mid-May) include 800,000 honey buzzards, close to 500,000 steppe buzzards, 75,000 steppe eagles, 30,000 black kites and 50,000 Levant sparrowhawks. Daily counts of 50,000 raptors are not uncommon, and in May 1985 no fewer than 220,000 honey buzzards were counted in one single day. In the autumn most species maintain a more northerly route along the Mediterranean Sea rather than the Red Sea. The exception is the steppe eagle, which is seen in similar, or even greater, numbers in the autumn. Mount Yoash, 2,297

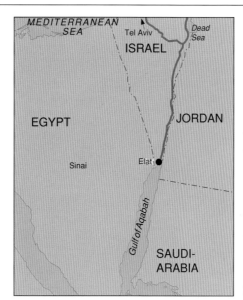

feet (700 m) above sea level, and 4 miles (6 km) west of Elat, is most of the time the best spot to view the raptors' spring migration. North Beach, east of the city, is best in the autumn. Although the desert around Elat at first sight seems to be barren, wildlife is relatively abundant. The general ban on hunting since the mid-1960s has favored animals such as the Dorcas gazelle and ibex. Both species occur commonly in the area today. Carnivores such as the gray wolf and hyena have also increased in number, but are mainly nocturnal and harder to catch a glimpse of. The hyrax is common in many wadis, but you have to be very lucky to spot one of the few remaining leopards.

Fauna of interest

MAMMALS: Ibex, Dorcas gazelle, mountain gazelle (Idmi), gray wolf, hyena, leopard, red fox, sand fox (Rüppel's fox), Blanford's fox, Fennec fox, hyrax, caracal, wild cat, cape hare, gerbil (Baluchistan gerbil).

BIRDS: Steppe eagle (February to mid-April, and late autumn), black kite (mid-March to mid-April), steppe buzzard (mid-March to mid-April), Levant sparrowhawk (end April), honey buzzard (end April to mid-May), Egyptian vulture, short-toed eagle, long-legged buzzard, greater and lesser spotted eagle, imperial eagle, booted eagle, Bonelli's eagle, osprey, 9 species of falcons, 3 species of harriers, black stork, some 60 locally breeding species and masses of migrants, ducks, waders and passerines.

Seasons

All year round, since different species migrate at different times and certain species are residents. The raptor migration is abundant from February to mid-May, with peaks at end February for the steppe eagle, end March to early April for the steppe buzzard and beginning of May for the honey buzzard. End October to beginning of November is good for the steppe eagle. Most waders pass

through in May. The desert climate is very hot and arid. Winter temperatures are tolerable, but May through September heat may be uncomfortable, with temperatures reaching 118°F (48°C). Humidity is always low. Rains are occasional but are always associated with flooding.

How to get there

International air service straight to Elat or to Tel Aviv, with domestic connection to Elat. Rental car, taxi or bike to commute between the city and Mount Yoash. It is convenient to alternate between different locations as the best spot to view the mainstream of migrating raptors may vary during the day. Up-to-date information about migration can be obtained at the International Birdwatching Center in downtown Elat.

Accommodation/food/camping

Large selection of hotels, eating-places and stores. For extended excursions into the Arava Valley there are hotels, youth hostels or accommodation in kibbutzes in several places along the Dead Sea and in Mizpe Ramon and Midreshet Ben Gurion in the Negev desert.

Other areas

Kefar Qassem, Israel, lies on the coastal plain inside Tel Aviv. Exceptionally large numbers of raptors pass through here during the autumn migration. It starts with honey buzzards (almost 400,000) in the beginning of September, followed by Levant sparrowhawks (30,000), accompanied by several other species at the end of the month. End September to early October is best, with lesser spotted eagles (100,000) and tens of thousands of pelicans. In addition, short-toed eagles (7,000), booted eagles (1,500), Egyptian vultures (300), red-footed falcons (2,000) and 25 other raptor species.

Bosporus, Turkey, at the narrow land bridge connecting Europe and Asia. About 100,000 migrant raptors pass here, from end August to beginning October. Honey buzzards (25,000), lesser spotted eagles (20,000), short-toed eagles (2,000), Levant sparrowhawks (5,000), black kites (2,500), booted eagles (500) and Egyptian vultures (500) are the most frequent. A total of some 20 species of raptors. White storks (300,000) and black storks (7,000) move through in August and early September. Best observation site is normally Buçuk Çamliça.

Çoruh Valley, northeastern Turkey, at the eastern shore of the Black Sea, is a rewarding place to watch migrating raptors from mid-September to mid-October. Autumn totals of close to 400,000, with single day's counts exceeding 50,000! Honey buzzards (140,000), black kites (6,000), steppe buzzards (200,000) and another 20 species of raptors, among them the saker falcon, imperial eagle, and greater and lesser spotted eagle. Simple accommodation in the city of Borçka, 103 miles (165 km) east of Trabzon.

CHRISTER FREDRIKSSON

The World's Richest Wildlife Areas
Serengeti National Park and
Ngorongoro Conservation Area, Tanzania

A leopard stretched along an umbrella acacia branch makes an elegant silhouette against the red morning sky. He is silent, but all around are the sounds of waking animals—the bellowing of wildebeests, snorting of buffalo, whinnying of zebras, the howling of a hyena and the distant roar of a lion.

As it grows lighter we see that the grassy savannah is dotted to the horizon with game. From the crest of a small hill, or "*kopje*," we observe tens of thousands of wildebeests, zebras, gazelles, buffalo and antelopes. From the next *kopje*, we see tens of thousands more. And there are more beyond that. In a day's safari you can encounter several hundred thousand animals. The abundance of wildlife is staggering; it amazes even those who have viewed the spectacle many times before.

In the open country, predators seek shade beneath the few trees or among the rocks. On one *kopje* lies a family of cheetahs, the world's fastest land animals. A female is suckling her cubs. There were five to start with, but now there are only three, and one has a bad limp. Maybe a hyena got them, or a lion. Cubs have many enemies.

Suddenly the mother spots something in the distance. Her gently maternal eyes gleam with the intensity of the hunter as they fasten on a Thomson's gazelle fawn a few hundred yards away. With tensed muscles, she shakes off the feeding cubs and creeps off,

crouching low. When she sees that the gazelle has an injured hind leg and can hardly walk, she relaxes and almost trots forward. In a burst of speed, she could reach 75 miles (120 km) an hour, but why bother?

She knocks over the fawn with her paw and squats beside it. The fawn gets up again, looks at its attacker and happily wags its tail. This is the first cheetah it has ever seen, and life is all a game to it. The cheetah grabs it by the neck and drags it back to her young. She will let it live for a while to accustom the cubs to living prey. Curious, but slightly nervous, they poke cautiously at the little doomed fawn.

For it, and for them, the childish games will soon be over, and they will face the realities of life and death in the Serengeti.

Their mother stares keenly at the horizon. No lion or leopard approaching?

Not yet.

The leopard (opposite page) climbs trees to avoid the flies at ground level and eat its prey in peace. It is reluctant to show itself in the daytime—unlike the cheetah, which is a typical diurnal animal.
The female cheetah goes hunting with her half-grown young, which accompany her until they are able to hunt for themselves. The Thomson's gazelle (above) is a favorite prey. When the cubs are quite small and she is still suckling them, the female lets them play with the prey before killing it (right).

The annual migration of wildebeest, or gnus (overleaf), fills the Serengeti savannahs with hundreds of thousands of them.

CHRISTER FREDRIKSSON

The giraffe is an out-and-out tree browser who prefers acacia scrub and gallery forest (above).

Thanks to poachers, African elephants with large tusks (left) are quite rare. Anyone buying ivory products, anywhere in the world, contributes to the extinction of the elephant.
Cattle egrets accompany elephants to catch insects disturbed by the their tramping.

The beak of the Rüppell's vulture is not strong enough to tear the tough hide of a wildebeest (second from left). If hyenas or the larger vultures do not get to the feast first, the vulture has to start with the soft parts around the mouth, eyes and tail.

Old-time big-game hunters rated the African buffalo (far left) one of the "Big Five" trophies a hunter should bring back from a safari. Others were the lion, leopard, elephant and rhinoceros.

The cheetah (left) is the sprinter of the savannah, built for swift dashes in open country. Early this century it was still to be found in deserts and semi-deserts from the Middle East to India.

Description

The Serengeti is an area of 11,584 square miles (30,000 sq km) in the borderland between Tanzania and Kenya. Roughly two-thirds of it have some level of protection, through the Serengeti National Park, the Ngorongoro Conservation Area, the Loliondo Controlled Area in Tanzania and the Masai Mara National Reserve in Kenya. The word "Serengeti" means "endless plains" in the Masai language, and the open, rolling grass savannahs in northwestern Tanzania live up to their name.

Serengeti is the location for the greatest of all wildlife spectacles on earth. Nowhere else is there to be found any similar concentration of game. Here live over 2 million ungulates of more than 30 species, and a wide array of carnivores, as well as over 500 bird species.

Serengeti National Park covers 5,700 square miles (14,760 sq km) and consists mainly of open grassland and tree savannah, dotted with inselberg hills (so-called *kopjes*) and gallery forests. It is crossed in all directions by several minor rivers. The area around Seronera was declared a reserve in 1929, and in 1951 the Serengeti National Park was created. The park is most famous for its almost incomprehensibly huge herds of wildebeests and zebras, as well as for its healthy population of lions.

Ngorongoro Conservation Area, NCA, covers 3,197 square miles (8280 sq km) and includes, apart from the famous crater, vast areas of savannah, semi-desert, mountain and forest. In the NCA lies also the famous Olduvai Gorge, with its excavation sites and finds of some of man's earliest ancestors, from 3.6 million years ago.

The Ngorongoro Crater itself is unique, difficult to give a fair description of in a few words only, but it is, to use a well-worn phrase, probably the closest one can get to the

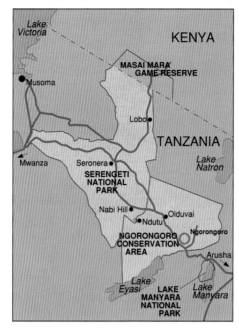

"Garden of Eden" on earth. The crater rim lies at an altitude of 7,546 feet (2300 m), and the sides drop dramatically 1,969 feet (600 m) to the almost flat crater floor, which measures just about 9 miles (15 km) in diameter. The latter is mostly wet grass savannah, with a large saline lake and small groves of tall fevertrees. This is one of the very few places left today where one still can see black rhinoceroses by the dozen. Luxuriant, lichen-covered montane forest grows along the crater rim and southwards/eastwards.

The animals of the crater stay here for most of the year, and do not migrate, as in the Serengeti. Another difference from the Serengeti is that the local Masai live here permanently. A number of Masai villages lie within the NCA, and their herdsmen have grazed cattle for hundreds of years in the excellent pastures of the area.

Fauna of interest

MAMMALS: Wildebeest (1.3 million), common zebra (200,000), Grant's gazelle (30,000), Thomson's gazelle (250,000), topi (50,000), impala (70,000), oribi, steenbok, klipspringer, Beisa oryx, eland, Defassa waterbuck, Bohor reedbuck, mountain reedbuck, bushbuck, roan antelope (SW Serengeti), hartebeest, Masai giraffe, Kirks dik-dik, African buffalo, elephant (Ngorongoro and Lobo), black rhinoceros (Ngorongoro only), hippopotamus, lion (1,500), leopard (especially around Seronera), cheetah, serval, hunting dog (Serengeti), spotted hyena, striped hyena, bat-eared fox, aardwolf, warthog, olive baboon, green vervet monkey, genets.

REPTILES: Nile crocodile, monitor lizard.

BIRDS: More than 500 species, among them: Masai ostrich, secretary bird, ground hornbill, marabou, white stork, Abdim's stork, crowned crane, martial eagle, species of vulture, bateleur, tawny eagle, long-crested eagle, Verraux's eagle owl, spotted eagle owl, bustard, sandgrouse, courser, kingfisher, bee-eater, flamingo, guineafowl, francolin, glossy starling, snake-eagle, roller, lapwing, hornbill, kite and 4 species of harrier.

Seasons

All year round. The driest season is between June and October. The rainy season is from November to May, with most rain during April and May. During the rainy season one finds the biggest concentrations of game in the areas around Nabi Hill, Ndutu and Gol Kopjes, where over a million large mammals can gather at the same time. As the drought advances from the south, the animals move north- and westwards, past Seronera and up toward Masai Mara, which they reach in July. There they stay until September. During June and July, the great migration is at its peak in the northern part of the Serengeti. In September/October, the herds start to return. June to December is best around Lobo. June to October is best in Seronera.

June and July are the coldest months, especially in the highlands of Ngorongoro. The landscape turns beautifully green during and after the rains, best in April/May, when the flowering plants are in their most vigorous bloom.

A male lion in the Serengeti. In a world constantly more densely populated, eco-tourism is one of the very few chances of survival for the great carnivores. If the African savannahs cannot provide wealth enough for local people through tourism, they will sooner or later be cultivated and their animals killed off.

Black rhinoceros in the Ngorongoro crater, one of the very few places where it is still to be seen in the wild.

How to get there

International flight to Arusha, thereafter 106 miles (170 km) to Ngorongoro, and a further 93 miles (150 km) to Seronera in the Serengeti. Small aircraft are available for flights to several of the landing strips within the reserves. In Arusha are several good safari outfitters and touring agencies that organize everything: tough truck expeditions, comfortable camping safari, and deluxe lodge safaris. Camping equipment and cars can be rented. At Seronera rides in hot-air balloons over the savannah are offered at dawn. In the Ngorongoro crater, only four-wheel-drive vehicles are permitted. Jeeps with drivers can be rented at the lodges there.

Accommodation/food/camping

Several lodges available: *Ndutu Lodge, Seronera Lodge, Sopa Lodge* and *Lobo Lodge* in the Serengeti. *Crater Lodge, Ngorongoro Wildlife Lodge, Rhino Lodge* and *Sopa Lodge* in the Ngorongoro. Public campsites available in: *Lobo, Bologonja, Seronera, Moru Kopjes, Kirawira, Ndutu* and *Nabi Hill*. Camping is not allowed in the Ngorongoro crater itself, only on the crater rim, at Simba Camp. One can also camp in other places than the public sites, but only with special permission.

Other areas

Selous Game Reserve, Tanzania. With an area of 19,770 square miles (51,200 sq km), it is the biggest wildlife reserve in Africa. Almost unexploited and uninhabited. Great herds of elephants and buffalo. Species as in the Serengeti, plus sable antelope and lesser kudu. Best July to March. Easiest to fly there. Several comfortable camps/lodges.

Tarangire National Park, Tanzania. 1,000 square miles (2600 sq km). Gently rolling plains with swamps, low mountain ranges, gallery forests and magnificent baobab-trees. Best during the dry season, June to October, when tens of thousands of ungulates gather along the Tarangire River. Species as in the Serengeti, plus lesser kudus and several local endemic birds.

Maasai Amboseli National Park, Kenya. 1,236 square miles (3200 sq km) One of the most beautiful national parks of Africa, having Mount Kilimanjaro's 19,685-foot (6000-m) peak in the background. Overexploited by tourism, but still rich in game and birds. Species as in the Serengeti, plus gerenuks and lesser kudus.

Maasai Mara National Reserve, Kenya. 645 square miles (1670 sq km). Has the highest density of game—and tourists—of any reserve in Kenya. Good all year round, but best July to September, when great numbers of the Serengeti wildebeest and zebra are here. Often the area north and west of the reserve has more game than the reserve itself. Species as in the Serengeti.

Samburu/Buffalo Springs/Shaba National Reserves, Kenya. 64/50/93 square miles (165/130/240 sq km) semi-desert and dense scrub bush, crossed by rivers. Species as in the Serengeti, plus reticulated giraffe, Grevy's zebra, Beisa oryx, gerenuk, Somali ostrich and several local species of birds.

Gombe National Park, Tanzania. 20 square miles (52 sq km) of forest at the shore of Lake Tanganyika, south of Kigoma. Jane Goodall has researched on the chimpanzees here for many years, and some flocks are quite used to people. Also red colubus, blue monkey and black-cheeked white-nosed monkey.

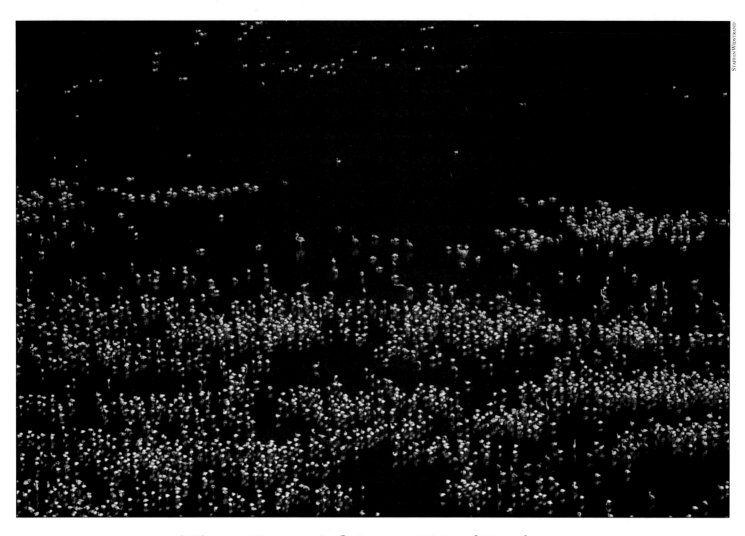

STAFFAN WIDSTRAND

Two East African Bird Lakes
Lake Nakuru National Park and Lake Naivasha, Kenya

Two million flamingos! More than you'll find anywhere else in the world. You cannot actually *see* two million flamingos all at one time. All you see, at first, is a vast pink blur coloring the fringe of Lake Nakuru, where they gather, not in flocks or colonies, but in entire nations. The mind cannot fully comprehend the magnitude of the assembly.

Seen through binoculars, the blur becomes a screen of dots—imagine a swarm of blackfly, but pleasantly pink. Venture closer and the dots become exotic flying creatures with long, slender necks, strange plankton-straining beaks and thin, vermilion legs.

American ornithologist Roger Tory Peterson called this "the world's most spectacular bird experience."

A thick salt crust cakes the shores of the lake, like frost despite the equatorial heat. It forms because the lake has no outlet, and all the salts rain-washed into it remain after evaporation. It is a *very* salt lake. The water feels thick and slippery, and it's warm, almost hot, because of the fierce sun above and the hot springs below this volcanic region.

This water is biological dynamite, exploding into a superabundant production of algae—the food for a long chain of creatures, from microscopic ciliates and small crustaceans to fish and flamingos. Thousands of tons of soupy blue-green algae are produced here daily, and the cichlid fish thrive on it, to become the main prey of the birds. In turn, many of the flamingos provide food for African fish eagles, jackals, hyenas and marabous.

One bird preys on another, and down on the ground earthbound enemies are always waiting. Weather may change the pattern of life and death. Heavy rains may dilute the saline water and kill the algae; when this happens some of the huge flamingo flocks move on to other salt lakes in the Great Rift Valley. But Lake Nakuru is never deserted. If only 200,000 pink birds remain, that's still a lot of flamingos.

"Naivasha" means "fresh water" in the Masai language, and Lake Naivasha is a green oasis in the dry landscape. In January, it is darkly flecked, almost black with ducks, cormorants and coots. Low over the water, flocks of terns dance like swarms of mosquitoes. In the tallest of the dead trees, colonies of white-breasted cormorants bustle about their business. There is an air shuttle of birds on their way to and from the lake's lavish smorgasbord. Tall goliath herons and crowned cranes of royal dignity stand in the shoreline belt of waving green papyrus. There are long-tailed cormorants with eyes of baleful red; malachite kingfishers glowing in their turquoise green; and lines of colorful ibises, storks and herons.

In a few hours at Naivasha or Nakuru, the visitor may see more birds than most people do in a lifetime. They are so numerous, so large, so richly colored, and usually so close, that the most hardened observer instantly turns into a bird-lover.

Lake Nakuru is a bird lake supreme. The white pelican (above) is there in the tens of thousands, the lesser flamingo (opposite) in hundreds of thousands. There is a lone greater flamingo in the picture. Some flamingos end up as a meal for the African fish eagle (below).

JAN PEDERSEN

The crowned crane (above) is a characteristic bird of freshwater wetlands throughout East Africa. It is closely related to the European crane, and common around Lake Naivasha. It is the national emblem of Uganda.

CHRISTER FREDRIKSSON

The malachite kingfisher, perched here in a stand of papyrus, is found near most watercourses in East Africa. Most are totally unafraid of man.

The piercing, gull-like call of the African fish eagle (right) is a typical sound of African bird lakes, and has been called the "Voice of Africa." Nearly fifty pairs breed around Lake Naivasha.

STAFFAN WIDSTRAND

Description

From north to south, straight across East Africa, runs the Great Rift Valley, an enormous fault fissure. On the valley floor lies, like pearls on a necklace, a band of shallow lakes, each quite different from the next, but all very rich in birdlife. The differences are mainly in the salinity of the water, which has a great influence on the ecology and selection of species.

Lake Nakuru is a true salt lake, world famous for its birdlife—especially the masses of flamingos, sometimes numbering up to 2 million (almost one-third of the world population of the lesser flamingo!), that congregate here. Lake Nakuru National Park was created in 1961 and was later expanded with assistance from the WWF to its present 77 square miles (200 sq km). The park includes not only the lake itself, but also parts of the lush surrounding fevertree forest and dry woodland savannah. Four hundred species of birds have been observed. During recent years black rhinoceroses have been reintroduced here, taken from other parts of Kenya where they were at greater risk of being killed by poachers.

The panoramic view from the dramatic cliffs of Baboon Rocks also provides good opportunities to see birds of prey.

Lake Naivasha, on the other hand, is a freshwater lake of some 58 square miles (150 sq km), with clear waters and, around its shores, dense stands of papyrus and fevertree. In spite of the lake having been tampered with by man—introduction of nutria, America crayfish, American black bass, salvinia and water hyacinth; using the lake water for irrigation; intense use of pesticides on the surrounding farms etc.—it is still a paradise for waterfowl. More than 400 bird species have been found. Birds can be counted here in the hundreds of thousands during wintertime, when many Eurasian migrants stay here. All land around the lake is privately owned, so the only access to the water for visitors is at the hotels and the campsites. In the lake lies *Crescent Island*, a private game reserve. Since there are no big carnivores there, visitors are permitted to walk around freely among the birds, zebras, Thomson's gazelles, bat-eared foxes and waterbucks.

Joy Adamson's home—now a museum, café and research station—also lies at the shores of Lake Naivasha. In its garden there is a fearless flock of black-and-white colobus monkeys and a pair of Verreaux's eagle-owls.

Fauna of interest

MAMMALS: Hippopotamus, Bohor reedbuck, common zebra, Masai giraffe, Defassa waterbuck, impala, Thomson's gazelle, Grant's gazelle, bat-eared fox. In *Lake Nakuru* also: Black rhinoceros (reintroduced), leopard, serval, spotted hyena, jackal, eland, bushbuck.

BIRDS: African fish eagle, osprey, Verreaux's eagle, bateleur, African hawk eagle, Lanner falcon, peregrine falcon, Verreaux's eagle-owl, spotted eagle-owl, crowned crane,

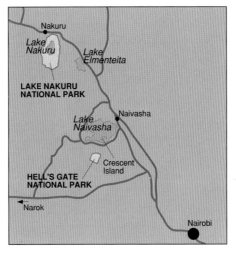

southern ground hornbill, purple gallinule, African jacana, African spoonbill, yellow-billed stork, woolly-necked stork, Abdim's stork, greater flamingo, lesser flamingo, saddle-bill stork, marabou, white pelican, pink-backed pelican, long-tailed cormorant, white-breasted cormorant, African darter, 12 species of heron, hammerkop, sacred ibis, Hadada ibis, secretary bird, ducks, geese, vultures, plovers/lapwings, stints, gulls, terns, pratincoles, sand plovers, lovebirds, bee-eaters, kingfishers, rollers, nightjars.

Seasons

All year round, but the hosts of migrants are only here in the winter, with greatest numbers in January/February. The long rains usually come in April/May, and the shorter rains in November/December. But the rain is no obstacle for visits. After the rains the landscape turns green. The numbers of flamingos vary irregularly.

How to get there

International flight to Nairobi, where there are probably more safari outfitters and touring agencies than in any other African city. They can organize everything from really tough expeditions to comfortable camping safaris and pure deluxe holidays. Lots of camping equipment and cars for hire. It is easy to drive, find the way and manage on one's own from Nairobi to Naivasha (53 miles/85 km) and Nakuru (93 miles/150 km).

Accommodation/food/camping

Naivasha: *Safariland Lodge* and *Lake Naivasha Hotel*. Several private campsites.

Nakuru: *Lake Nakuru Lodge, Lion Hill Camp.* Several public campsites.

Other areas

Hell's Gate National Park, Kenya, lies adjacent to Lake Naivasha and is an arid scrubland area, containing a great ravine, with steep basaltic cliffs and volcanic sulfurous springs. Colonies of vultures. Also Verreaux's eagles, lammergeiers, peregrine falcons, Lanner fal-

cons, rock hyraxes, klipspringers, common zebras, red hartebeests, steenboks, and sometimes cheetahs or lions. Campsite only.

Lake Baringo, Kenya, is a shallow freshwater lake with muddy water, situated in the arid semi-desert north of Bogoria. Main attractions are the hippos, crocodiles, herons, storks and other waterfowl. Lodge, tented camp and campsite.

Lake Bogoria National Reserve, Kenya. As salty as but not yet as famous as Lake Nakuru. Here are often more flamingos than in Nakuru, but not the same variety or numbers of other waterfowl. The lake is surrounded by a number of hot springs with boiling water and squirting mud, and it lies in a hot and arid landscape. The reserve comprises 41 square miles (107 sq km) and was created mainly to protect the elusive greater kudus that live here.

Lake Manyara National Park, Tanzania, includes about one-third of the lake and its immediate surroundings, most famous for its tree-climbing lions and masses of flamingos and other waterbirds. Also elephants, buffalo, hippopotamuses, silvery-cheeked hornbills, and martial eagles. *Lake Manyara Lodge,* public bungalows and three public campsites.

Parc National de Djoudj, Senegal. 62 square miles (160 sq km) of lakes and marshes. Vast numbers of breeding white pelicans, and breeding, migrating and wintering waterbirds. Best December to April. Boat trips. One lodge.

Réserve de Moulay Bousselham, Morocco. 35 square miles (90 sq km) of the delta where the river Qued Drader reaches the Atlantic, including the lagoon Merdja Zerga, close to the village Moulay Bousselham. A migration- and wintering-ground for hundreds of thousands of waterbirds from all over Europe. Flamingos, storks, cormorants, herons, shorebirds, coots, ducks, terns, slender-billed curlews, Cape marsh owls, peregrine falcons, long-legged buzzards, marbled ducks, pratincoles. Good all year round, best in winter. Camping and small hotels/pensions.

Blacksmith plover

STEFAN WIDSTRAND

STAFFAN WIDSTRAND

Game-Rich Savannahs and Luxuriant Wetlands
Chobe National Park and
the Okavango Delta, Botswana

It is a still, starry night on the dry savannahs of Chobe. A deep roar outside my tent startles me awake. I jerk bolt-upright and feel the hair on the back of my neck rise.

Five feet (1.5 m) away a full-grown male lion is silhouetted against the next tent. I learn what "cold shivers down the spine" feel like, and it is not pleasant. The lion lets out his territorial roar—a sound that on a calm night can be heard for miles. Close up, it is utterly terrifying. Of

In the dense acacia scrub, the lions of Chobe and the Okavango delta hunt giraffes, but in open terrain they prefer zebras and impalas. The male lion that gave voice so mightily in the night (above) marks out his territory partly with his roars, partly by leaving his scent on bushes and grass.

course, I know the roar is not intended for me, but for any interested lionesses in the area, and possible rival males. It says, "Here I am, if anyone wants to make something of it." But that's rational thinking. With the great beast just outside your mosquito net, you don't think rationally.

I get out my little pocket knife, determined to sell my life dearly. But the lion doesn't want to take it, or to eat me. He moves off, breathing heavily.

I hear more roars, each farther away, then I am alone once more with the starry sky and the chorus of crickets.

When you get close to them, many large animals turn out to be smaller than you pictured them. Not so the lion: he's bigger.

He is phenomenally strong; he can gallop very fast

41

for short distances, and leap high obstacles while carrying heavy prey in his mouth.

He is the King of Beasts, an international symbol of courage, but there are conflicting reports about his bravery. Those who know lions say they are much like other creatures, including humans, in this respect. Some are braver than others.

An ill-fed, hungry lion is bolder than a well-fed one. And, like most big animals, they will keep to themselves unless you molest them. The rare man-eaters are usually old lions who no longer have the strength to chase and kill their natural prey such as antelope or zebra.

Common zebra (above) on the dry Chobe savannahs. Each has its individual stripe pattern. There are many theories on why zebras have stripes, but no real answer.

The acacias are leguminous, and the most characteristic trees of the African savannahs. This example is near Savuti, in Chobe National Park.

Okavango

Papyrus—everywhere swaying papyrus and floating waterlilies. We have moved on from the dry plains of Chobe to the well-watered greenery of the Okavango delta.

Narrow winding channels, interspersed with stretches of open water, form a gigantic natural labyrinth. We paddle a canoe, drive a motorboat and punt our way through the cool, clear and, in fact, drinkable water of the Okavango delta. If boatmen from the baTawana tribe had not shown us the way, we would have been lost in half an hour. In the Okavango, one place is deceptively like another. But something new waits around every bend. The rumbling grunts of a hippopotamus are heard, and its wash surges around the papyrus beds as it pushes its way through the vegetation. An elephant stands close to the edge, squirting water over itself with its trunk.

Then, with massive dignity, it withdraws to firm ground. Crocodiles bigger than our canoe interrupt their sunbathing, slide swiftly into the water and disappear. Overhead fly waterfowl—herons, ibises, eagles, storks, darters, kingfishers, ducks, geese and waders.

Surprisingly, all this greenery exists on the edge of the Kalahari desert, a vast expanse of red sand where thousands of early travelers died of thirst.

The Okavango delta is formed where the great river flows into the sands of the Kalahari desert, finally disappearing into a sea of papyrus and waterlilies (above).

The hippopotamus (below) is common. Its meat is good to eat, and many African game wardens believe it could become one of the continent's biggest natural sources of protein.

When elephants gather, big is beautiful (next page).

Description

In the semi-arid and sparsely populated borderlands between Namibia, Zimbabwe and Botswana lies a complex of national parks and nature reserves that is one of the richest wild-life regions in all of Africa, second only to the East African savannahs. Huge herds of zebras, wildebeests and various antelopes migrate seasonally in search of fresh pasture and water—a complicated system depending on if, when and where the rains will fall. They are followed by all kinds of carnivores, birds of prey and carrion eaters.

The biggest threats to this fragile and an-cient system, built on mobility and migration, are the two enormously long wildlife fences that have been erected straight across the migration routes, to prevent the wildlife from mingling with the domestic cattle. The aim is to minimize the risk to cattle of being infected with hoof-and-mouth disease. The fences effectively cut off the animals' traditional migration and hence have already caused the deaths of hundreds of thousands of zebras, wildebeests and antelopes.

The Okavango delta is one of Africa's few greater, yet still unexploited water systems, ironically, thanks to a fiery little insect—the tse-tse fly, often called "the best game warden of Africa." This insect transmits a fatal disease called "Nagana" to cattle, so where the fly lives all cattle-keeping is impossible. Wildlife, on the other hand, is immune and does not get the disease at all.

The Okavango River runs from the highlands of Angola, but instead of heading for the Atlantic, a mere 186 miles (300 km) away, it runs some 620 miles (1000 km) straight across southern Africa, and then disappears into the sands of the Kalahari desert (at 965 300 square miles/2.5 million sq km, the largest sand area on earth), creating an inland delta of some 5,792 square miles (15 000 sq km). The delta has river forks, channels, lakes, islands by the thousands and vast areas of papyrus swamp. On solid ground are gallery forests of mopane trees, various palms and camel-thorn trees. An area of the delta measuring 1,920 square miles (5000 sq km) is protected through the Moremi Wildlife Reserve, created by the local ba-Tawana people on their own initiative in 1962.

One of the most important ecological factors in the delta is the annual inundation, following the rainy season in Angola. Some years the water reaches as far as the enigmatic Lake Ngami, or even to desertlike Makgadik-gadi or Nxai Pans. Lake Ngami is very rich in birds and in October to March normally has ducks and geese in the hundreds of thousands.

Chobe National Park covers an area of 7,270 square miles (11 700 sq km) and borders the Caprivi Game Park of Namibia. It mainly consists of scrub-, tree- and grassland savannah, dotted with *inselbergs/kopjes*, mopane forests and papyrus swamps (at the Linyanti and Chobe rivers). In years with heavy rain, even the Savuti Channel holds

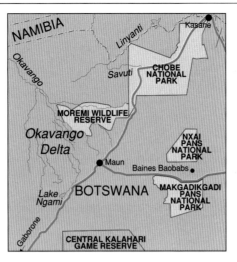

water, and then during the dry season attracts vast numbers of game. Especially impressive are the herds of elephants, larger than almost anywhere in Africa today. On several of the *inselbergs/kopjes* are found ancient rock paint-ings, picturing the wildlife of bygone days, probably painted sometime between 1000 and 1800 A.D., by the local Kung-bushmen.

Nxai Pans National Park. Open grass savannah, surrounded by arid scrub, in semi-desert surroundings. Here is also a periodic salt lake. Good area for viewing cheetah, spring-bok and gemsbok.

Makgadikgadi Pans Game Reserve. A minor part of the huge former Lake Mak-gadikgadi (larger than Lake Victoria). Most years the area is completely dry and seemingly empty of wildlife, but after heavy rains it receives some water and suddenly comes very much alive—algae, plankton, fish, and all kinds of creatures preying on these. Banes Baobabs lies between Makgadikgadi and Nxai Pans and is an ancient cult site. The few baobabs here are the only larger trees for hundreds of miles and the place is truly enchanted.

Fauna of interest

MAMMALS: Lechwe, sitatunga (Okavango), African buffalo, hippopotamus, lion, leopard, cheetah, serval, spotted hyena, brown hyena, aardwolf, hunting dog, greater kudu, Chap-man's zebra, wildebeest, eland, white rhino-ceros, steenbok, springbok (Makgadikgadi and Nxai Pans), gemsbok (Nxai Pans), bat-eared fox, common waterbuck, puku (Chobe), impala, tsesseby (Topi), African elephant (herds of more than 500!), giraffe, sable ante-lope (Chobe), Cape pangolin, roan antelope, common reedbuck, spotted-necked otter, Chacma baboon.

BIRDS: 450 breeding species. Seven species of stork, sacred ibis, African darter, white pelican, wattled crane, spur-winged goose, Egyptian goose, ten species of eagle, Lanner falcon, Pel's fishing owl, African jacana, secretary bird, ostrich, greater flamingo, lesser flamingo, pygmy goose, African skimmer, southern ground hornbill, parrots, bee-eaters,

kingfishers, hornbills, herons, vultures, bustards, sand grouse, pratincoles, owls.

REPTILES: Nile crocodile, monitor lizard.

Seasons

Best time for visits is April to October. November to March is the rainy season. In April the rains are over, the landscape is green, but the animals are widely dispersed. In October the heat comes close to 104°F (40°C), it is very dry and the animals are concentrated around the few existing waterholes. Impressive numbers of game in limited areas. Highest water levels in the delta are July to October. Coolest temperatures (c. 77°F/ 25°C daytime and 41°F/5°C nighttime) in June to August.

How to get there

International flight to Gaborone (Botswana), Windhoek (Namibia) or Harare (Zimbabwe). Local flight or bus/car to Maun.

Accommodation/food/camping

A number of excellent lodges in the Okavango delta and in Chobe National Park. Several good local touring agencies in Maun that also arrange comfortable camping expeditions. Some even offer elephant rides in the Oka-vango, the only area in Africa where this is done. Excursions in mokoros (dugout canoes) and motorboat trips are arranged from most lodges, for instance, to visit the great heronries. For people traveling in their own four-wheel-drive vehicle and camping (equipment can be rented in Maun), there are public or private campsites outside Maun, in Chobe and in the delta.

Other areas

Hwangie National Park, Zimbabwe. Comprising 5,020 square miles (13 000 sq km). This, the finest of Zimbabwe's national parks, is easiest reached via Victoria Falls. Visits permitted only in the northern third. Arid savannah and gallery forests. Same species as in Chobe—white rhinoceros, sable antelope, greater kudu being the most interesting. Several observation platforms at waterholes.

Etosha National Park, Namibia, is one of the best game reserves of Africa. Comprising 8,600 square miles (22 270 sq km) of desert, semi-desert, open savannah and periodic salt lakes. Holds the densest population of lions in the continent, and species like caracal, black rhinoceros, greater kudu, damara dik-dik, black-nosed impala and blue crane, as well as the species of Chobe.

Kruger National Park, South Africa, comprising 7,512 square miles (19 455 sq km). An area easy to get around in and with good roads. Open tree savannah country, crossed by rivers. Hunting dog, bushbuck, lion, leopard, spotted hyena, cheetah, elephant, giraffe, hippo, greater kudu, white rhinoceros, roan antelope. Good all year round; best August to October.

KRISTINA LIND

KRISTINA LIND

Island of Lemurs and Chameleons
Madagascar

The smell of damp earth, smoke, and dewy grass permeates the mountain rainforest reserve of Périnet. A peculiar call rings out from the trees. Sometimes it sounds like a crying child, sometimes a police siren, or even the song of whales.

It is the morning cry of the indri, a species of lemur. Males and females give a dawn concert together. Their young join in, and from the distance other indri families answer. "Indri" means "look there" in Malagasy. The scientist who first described the species believed his guide had given him the actual name of the animal, so that is what he called it. The Madagascans actually call it the "babacoata," which means "duffer." It is looked upon as a sort of stupid human ancestor who stayed up in the trees and remained a monkey. Verreaux's sifaka is another species of lemur which lives in the drier forests and is an excellent climber and leaper from branch to branch. It is the best-known lemur, and a favorite star of wildlife films. Its ground movements can be comical—bouncing along, with sideways hops, skips and jumps, while wildly waving its long arms above its head.

Lemurs are a remarkable family of prosimians, distantly related to monkeys, and found only on Madagascar and the little Comoro group of islands. Linnaeus named them "lemur" after the terrifying ghosts of Roman times, which had similar glowing

ANDERS HAGLUND

eyes. Thirty species live here—from the indri, nearly 3 feet (1 m) tall, down to the mouse lemur, not much bigger than the palm of your hand. Twelve other lemur species—the largest of them the size of a mountain gorilla—have been exterminated by man in the last thousand years. Their skeletal remains have been found during archeological digs, along with shards of the pots they were cooked in. Other species which have disappeared include giant land tortoises, a huge bird, the size of an ostrich, with no wings but enormous feet, and a lizard nearly 70 feet (21.3 m) long.

Still in existence, but threatened, are more than 800 kinds of butterfly, a Madagascar moth which produces valuable silk, and more types of chameleon than can be found anywhere else.

Madagascar is unique, containing habitats and life forms that exist nowhere else. Its plants and animals have evolved in their own way for more than a hundred million years —the time scientists believe the island has been separated from the African mainland. Ninety percent of its animal species and 85 percent of its plants are unique to Madagascar. If habitats are commercially exploited, these species will disappear forever.

A group of lemurs sit basking in the morning sun, their backs to a rock. With arms and legs wide apart they squint up at the sun.

They do not look like terrifying ghosts. They appear friendly—some lemurs have been tamed and kept as pets—but they could all become ghosts if their territory is further despoiled.

Even as they sit there, logging goes on at a furious pace all around them. Bit by bit their forests are being destroyed.

Their future depends on whether eco-tourism makes these irreplaceable forests more commercially valuable than sacks of charcoal.

The ring-tailed lemur, or catta (above), is known as the "sun-worshipping lemur."

A female black lemur in Nosy Comba (opposite above) is curious, but obviously nervous.

Half of the world's chameleon species (opposite below) are found only on Madagascar. They live in all kinds of habitats, but are most easily found among the orchid-covered trees and shrubs of the rainforest.

KRISTINA LIND

Over 85 percent of Madagascar's original forest land has been cut, and the devastation is proceeding at a horrifying pace. When the forest cover is gone, the fertile soil soon disappears with the rain. North of Ambositra (above), there was dense forest only a few decades ago. Verreaux's sifaka (below), in Amboasary Sud, got its name from its call, which sounds like a sneeze (sifakh!).

The Madagascans believe that chameleons (right) are unhappy human souls. Causing the death of a chameleon brings catastrophe. The island's largest chameleon grows to nearly 28 inches (70 cm) in length.

ANDERS HAGLUND

KRISTINA LIND

Description

Madagascar is the fourth-largest island in the world and, at 227,817 square miles (590 000 sq km), is slightly bigger than France. The interior is dominated by highlands, which in the east descend abruptly to narrow coastal plains. Most of the east and north were originally covered by rainforest, which is today replaced by paddy-fields and grazing lands. In the south and west, the drier climate has created dry forests, semi-desert and grass savannahs with baobab trees. The forests decrease every year, both in drier and rainier areas, mostly due to cultivation and the gathering of wood for fuel. During the 2,000 years of human habitation here, more than 85 percent of the original forest cover has disappeared. This makes soil erosion a continuously more serious problem in great parts of the country. Wide areas once covered by luxuriant rainforest are now eroded down to the sterile clay, and nothing can be cultivated there. The local climate has turned drier in many areas.

Several biotopes are to be found only on Madagascar, among them the dry Didieria thorntree forests in the south.

The nature areas most worth visiting are:

Réserve Faunale de Périnet-Analomazoatra lies halfway along the railway between Antananarivo and the east coast. Comprising 3 square miles (8 sq km) of rainforest, at an altitude of 3,280 feet (1000 m). The best place to see lemurs such as indri, diadem sifaka and red-fronted lemur, and fossa, tenrecs, Madagascar banded kestrels, Madagascar kestrels and several other endemic species of birds. Many chameleons. Knowledgeable guides and good lodging at the railway station. Night walks with guide. The best parts of this rainforest lie farthest away from the tracks.

Berenty, 50 miles (80 km) west of Fort Dauphin. Private reserve, less than 0.5 square miles (1 sq km)(!), but still probably the most visited in the island. Dry forest with fearless lemurs that can be fed by hand—ring-tailed lemur, Verreaux's sifaka, brown lesser mouse-lemur, sportive lemur and a colony of Madagascar flying foxes—and 56 bird species. One of the best dry-forest areas. A bit arranged and parklike.

Amboasary Sud. Private reserve close by Berenty, with the same biotope and species, but with fewer visitors and less parklike.

Bezaha – Mahafaly. WWF reserve in the unique Didieria thorntree forest, southeast of Tuléar. Verreaux's sifaka, ring-tailed lemur. Ox-cart from the village of Betioky. Simple lodging. Bring your own food.

Parc National Montagne d'Ambre. Comprising 70 square miles (182 sq km) of virgin rainforest, outside Antsiranana, in the north. Sandford's lemur, crowned lemur, fossa. Good hiking trails.

Parc National Ranomafana, at Fianarantsoa. Dense rainforest with rich wildlife, for example, the golden bamboo lemur, discovered first in 1987 (!). Camping. Good trails. Good guides in the park headquarters.

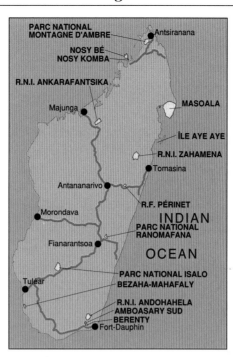

Île Aye Aye, Rogers Island. Small island with a private coconut farm. Here can be found some of the remaining specimens of the Aye-aye—a strange animal that occupies the ecological niche of the woodpeckers, of which there are none in Madagascar. Lodging on the mainland. Daily boat trips arranged. Reached via Fenoarivo Atinarana, north from Tomasina Mananarava, entrance at Antongi Bay.

Nosy Komba is a small island off the north-western coast of Madagascar. Black lemurs here are very tame, and it is somewhat of a tourist trap. Lodging available. Boat from Antsahampano, or from the tourist-exploited neighboring island Nosy Bé, which can be reached by plane. On Nosy Bé lies the reserve *Lokobe*, which has black lemurs and Madagascar fish eagles. The island *Nosy Tanikely* is a marine reserve and has black lemurs, Madagascar flying foxes, white-tailed tropicbirds and fine coral reefs with good snorkeling/diving.

The Masoala Peninsula in the northeast is the largest untouched rainforest region in the island. The area is without roads, but has trails for tough hiking. A national park to be, probably home to several yet undescribed species. Some species thought to be extinct have been rediscovered here.

Parc National Isalo. Comprising 315 square miles (815 sq km) of canyons with strange rock-formations, in the dry lands northeast of Tuléar. Verreaux's sifakas warming themselves in the morning sun, brown lemurs, ring-tailed lemurs and fossas. Lemurs mainly in the oases. Long hikes and camping necessary. Guides and porters in the village of Ranohira.

Réserve Naturelle Intégrale de Ankara-fantsika. Comprising 232 square miles (602 sq km) of dry lowland forest, southeast of the town Majunga. Diadem sifaka, Verreaux's sifaka, brown lemur, mongoose lemur, Milne-

Edward's sportive lemur, woolly lemur, fossa and a host of endemic birds, such as the Madagascar crested ibis. Camping.

Réserve Naturelle Intégrale de Zahamena. At 301 square miles (780 sq km), east of the Ambatondrazaka, the largest rainforest reserve on Madagascar. Indri and ruffed lemur.

Réserve Naturelle Intégrale de Andohahela. Comprising 301 square miles (780 sq km), north-west of Fort Dauphin, covering rainforest, dry forest and arid bushland. Rich fauna, including fossa, 14 species of lemur and 100 bird species.

Fauna of interest

Thirty species of lemur and 8 species of carnivores exist on the island. Fossa, falanouc and fanaloka belong to the Viverridae family, and the other carnivores belong to the mongoose family, Herpestidae.

No wildcats, foxes, wolves or mustelids exist here. Tenrecs are to be found only on Madagascar. There are 256 bird species, almost all of them endemic, and as many as 5 of the bird families are endemic. So are 225 out of 235 species of reptiles. Here live also more than half of the world's species of chameleons.

Seasons

The rainy season is November to May, and is at its worst December to February. Then virtually all roads are impassable. The east coast can be hit by tropical cyclones, with heavy rain and hard winds several days in a row, at any time of the year. May to September/October is best for visiting. June to August is winter, and hence it is cooler in the highlands, with the risk of night frost.

How to get there

International flight to Antananarivo. Domestic flight (the only possible method during the rainy season) or bus/taxi/rented car within the country. There are two shorter railroads. Transportation is a problem in many places. It continues to be difficult to obtain permission to visit Réserves Naturelles Intégrales, although this is now said to be changing. Permits through Direction des Eaux et Forêts in Antananarivo.

Other areas

The Seychelles. 115 islands, clustered in the Indian Ocean. On Aride Island more than 160,000 pairs of terns of six different species breed—among them the elegant fairy tern. On the sandy Bird Island 2 million sooty terns breed—one of the densest colonies of birds anywhere. Mahé and Praslin are home to several endemic bird species. At sea, frigatebirds, shearwaters, noddies, sooty terns, fairy terns, masked boobies and white-tailed tropicbirds can often be sighted.

Aldabra is a group of coral islands, 59 square miles (153 sq km) in size, belonging to the Seychelles. Here live tens of thousands of Aldabra giant tortoises, about a million frigatebirds and thousands of red-footed boobies.

STEFAN WIDSTRAND

Mountain Gorillas and Hippos
Parc National des Virunga, Zaïre

The nearer we come to the cloud-covered volcanoes, the more the African road shrinks into a muddy track. Coffee, bananas, pawpaw and sugar cane are grown in what once was rainforest. In the villages, cheery children rush forward and wave to us. Their mothers wave, too, despite the buckets of water or bunches of bananas on their heads. At the last village the road ends, and we pitch our tents.

Here the bamboo and the mountain rainforest begin. This is Djomba, at the foot of the volcanoes in Virunga National Park, in eastern Zaïre.

Early next morning we hike up to mountain-gorilla territory. We are accompanied by park rangers Sebagabo and Banga, who visit the gorillas every day, even when there are no tourists to admire them. The gorillas move no more than a couple of hundred yards a day as they browse in the bamboos, so the rangers always know where to find them.

Suddenly the undergrowth in front of us is torn aside, and there he stands—440 pounds (200 kg) of mountain gorilla literally an arm's length away! His human-looking eyes examine us carefully. All is peaceful and unthreatening. He grunts a couple of short greeting phrases, to which our guides reply. They have practically been adopted by the gorillas and know their language.

The big one turns and vanishes into the bamboo, loudly informing his troop that the guides are back with a new bunch of tourists. We follow him and enter a clearing in the thicket the size of an average living room. We learn the big fellow is called Rugabo, and is one of the three largest "silverbacks" among the four hundred mountain gorillas that still survive in the wilds. A silver-gray back designates a leader.

Some thirty gorillas of all ages are lying down, climbing, sitting, crawling about, eating and sleeping. They are curious, but reserved. The youngsters chase one

STAFFAN WIDSTRAND

another through the thicket, while Rugabo and the older females sit in dignity, chewing bamboo shoots. Soon the small ones let their curiosity get the better of them and cannot help examining the visitors. Small gorilla fingers feel the cloth of trousers and camera bags, and we must back away, for park rules insist we stay 5 yards (5 m) from the gorillas.

Of course, you want to pick up the infants and cuddle them, but this is no zoo and it is strictly forbidden even to touch one. The reason, in part, is that no one knows how its parents might react, but mainly it is to prevent our infecting them with human diseases. Mountain gorillas can catch almost all of them, and an epidemic of whooping cough, pneumonia, measles or the common cold would soon wipe out the whole species. So don't visit them if you have a cold.

We sit for an hour near this family of gorillas in their "living room." They are unbelievably like us and they, too, feel that we are closer to them than to any other animals. They know there is something special about us. No other animal would be tolerated so close to a gorilla family; no other animal would be so trusted. Rugabo has shown complete composure by lying on his back, yawning, breaking wind and sleeping—only five yards away. When we move on, he looks up and grunts a farewell.

Most gorillas are shy, so we were surprised to be accepted so readily by Rugabo and his family.

Mountain gorillas were first discovered by explorers in 1903, in what was then the Belgian Congo. They have longer and thicker fur than the West African kind, and it protects them from the cold at altitudes of around 10,000 feet (3050 m).

Although closely related to the chimpanzee, gorillas are far bigger—the largest of the anthropoid, or "manlike," apes. When they stand erect they are up to 5.5 feet (1.7 m) tall. The adults seldom climb trees, and every night the gorillas build new sleeping nests on the ground.

The only place in the world where mountain gorillas

Look but don't touch—gorilla tourism in practice (above).

Visits to the gorillas are well organized, and disturbing the animals is kept to a minimum, so the big male gorilla can relax (below).

still survive is around the Virunga volcanoes, a region shared by three of the poorest countries in the world— Rwanda, Zaïre and Uganda. The thought strikes us that, if tourists' money had not made the gorillas more valuable alive than dead, they would now be dead, or sold into captivity in zoos.

Thanks to the work of WWF and the Frankfurt Zoological Association, they are still with us and, for the first time since they were discovered, increasing in numbers, slowly but surely. They are now the pride of their three nations. We see football teams, schools, bars and restaurants named after the best-known of the male gorillas, and in Djomba all the tough little boys call themselves "Rugabo" rather than "Rambo" or "The Terminator." Hundreds of people have found work through gorilla tours, and poaching has diminished radically.

But around the Virunga Mountains the human population is growing by 3 to 4 percent annually. The present conflict, the cause of such large-scale human suffering, adds further poignancy to the question: How long will there be space for the gorillas?

STAFFAN WIDSTRAND

On foot among the Virunga volcanoes, the home territory of the mountain gorilla. The trees in the mountain rainforests are low and wholly overgrown with lichen, moss and climbing plants. Here, and in the bamboo zone farther down, is where these large, peaceable animals thrive.

Although normally a peaceful herbivore, the hippopotamus is one of the most dangerous species in Africa. Many people are injured or killed every year while swimming or traveling by boat in hippo territory. This happens when they disturb courting or young animals, or frighten hippos feeding on land. Along the Rutshuru River (right), there are more than 15,000— probably the world's densest concentration of hippos.

STAFFAN WIDSTRAND

Description

The Zaïrian part of the Virunga volcanic territory is part of the Parc National des Virunga. Formed in 1925, it is the oldest national park in Africa. In Zaïre it covers more than 3,080 square miles (8000 sq km) and contains also the plains of Rwindi, Rutshuru and Ishango, which are rich in wildlife; part of the Ruwenzori Mountains (the Mountains of the Moon); and the shores of Lake Idi Amin.

The landscape is very varied, comprising open grass savannahs, wood savannahs, gallery forests, riverbanks, wetlands, lakeshores, rainforests, mountain rainforests and Afro-alpine moors. The highest of the Virungas is Karisimbi, at 14,787 feet (4507 m); in the Ruwenzoris, Mount Stanley rises to 18,340 feet (5590 m).

Visits like those to the gorillas can be made to a large group of chimpanzees in the Tongo forest. They are slightly shyer than the gorillas, but they are maybe even closer to human beings. Tourism to visit the chimpanzees has only just begun. Several groups live in the region and will probably become accustomed to being visited.

The Rutshuru River runs through the southern part of the park; it is probably the watercourse in Africa that contains the most hippopotamuses. No other natural environment in the world produces more mammal flesh in such a limited area—more than 15,000 hippos live along this relatively short stretch of river. Where the river enters Lake Idi Amin, it has created a veritable bird paradise that contains most of the African wetland species. At Rwindi, south of the lake, the landscape opens onto large grass savannahs teeming with wildlife. Tens of thousands of Kob antelopes graze here and involuntarily provide the many lions of the region with their daily food. In addition, thanks to the ban on the ivory trade, the elephant population has begun slowly to recover from the violent and horribly effective illegal hunting of the 1980s.

Fauna of interest

Mountain forests:
MAMMALS: Mountain gorilla (only in Virunga and the Djomba area), leopard, chimpanzee, blue monkey, black-and-white colubus, olive baboon, African buffalo, giant forest hog, green vervet monkey.

BIRDS: White-naped raven, crowned hawk eagle, trogons, sunbirds and several local passerines.

Plains, rivers and lowland forests:
MAMMALS: Olive baboon, green vervet monkey, black-and-white colubus, L'Hoest's monkey, chimpanzee, lion (many in Rwindi), leopard, serval, spotted hyena, striped hyena, aardvark, bat-eared fox, elephant (reduced from 30,000 in 1972 to 800 in 1992), buffalo, Kob antelope (tens of thousands, the most common antelope), okapi (rarely seen, northern parts of the park), bongo, common

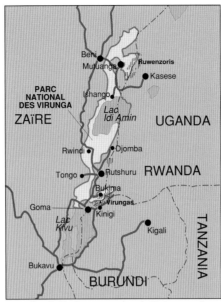

waterbuck, Defassa waterbuck, Bohor reedbuck, topi, sitatunga, bushbuck, giant forest hog, warthog, hippopotamus, several species of mongoose, civet and genet.

BIRDS: Crowned crane, marabou, saddlebill stork, whale-headed stork (rarely seen), African fish eagle, African spoonbill, peregrine falcon, white pelican, sacred ibis, gray parrot, painted snipe, great blue turaco, Egyptian goose, shorebirds, kingfishers, weavers, sunbirds, herons, raptors and vultures.

REPTILES: Nile monitor lizard, rock python, Nile crocodile.

Seasons

All year round. Rainfall is heavy from September to December, and from March to May, but even then visits are feasible to both the mountain gorillas and the lowland areas.

How to get there

The very tragic and chaotic situation on the border between, and in, Rwanda and eastern Zaïre has of course influenced gorilla tourism in the region. Tourism here today is a mere fraction of what it was before 1994. Between Goma and Djomba there have been four gigantic refugee camps since 1994. Several gorillas have been killed since 1995. But still, all the infrastructure for gorilla tourism is in place again, for the adventurous traveler.

Goma can be reached by domestic flight from Kinshasa, by international flights from Nairobi or Bujumbura, or by main road through Uganda and Rwanda/Burundi. There are hotels, efficient local tour operators and the local headquarters of the National Parks administration (IZCN), where gorilla permits are issued. Queues to get them without advance booking can be long. The gorillas are reached most easily through Bukima village (two to three hours north of Goma) or Djomba village (four hours north of Goma). Organized gorilla tourism has existed here for several years. Similar arrangements for visiting the

chimpanzees may be made at, for instance, Tongo, two hours north of Goma. In each case a permit is valid for a single one-hour visit; they are very expensive in all three countries.

The Ruwenzoris are most easily visited from Kasese, in Uganda; Mutuanga, the alternative in Zaïre, is reached after one or two days' travel from Goma.

Accommodation/food/camping

There are several hotels in Goma and well-stocked shops and markets. Djomba has a lodge—and a very basic cabin. Bukima has a similar cabin. Camping outside the villages is possible. Tongo has a lodge. At Rwindi there is the luxurious Rwindi Lodge, where no camping is permitted.

Other areas

Bwindi Impenetrable Forest National Park, Uganda. At present (1997) this is the safest, most easily accessible and convenient location for mountain-gorilla tourism. Here are some 220 gorillas in dense forest, and 3 or 4 groups are habituated to visitors. Very well organized. Hotel and simple lodging available.

Mgahinga Gorilla National Park, Uganda. Mountain-gorilla tourism is now well organized here.

Kibale Forest National Park, Uganda. Lowland and mountain rainforest. Chimpanzees that are trained to accept visitors. Eleven species of monkeys.

Parc National des Volcans, Rwanda. Several groups of mountain gorillas can be visited from the center in Kinigi. The Kinigi gorillas are surely the most visited; this is where Dian Fossey conducted her pioneering studies. Together with the Zaïre park, this complex of national parks is one of the finest protected areas in Africa.

A result of the mountain gorilla project is local pride in the animals. Bars, restaurants, brothels and, as here, a Catholic school for girls are named after the large males.

Orangutan!
Danum Valley Conservation Area, Sabah (Borneo), Malaysia

Calmly and purposefully the big, red-haired anthropoid ape moves from branch to branch in the strangler-fig tree. She is eating her way methodically through the figs. There is no screaming or chattering. She makes no daredevil leaps. The orangutan is no ordinary monkey.

After eating for several hours, she settles down on a large branch to rest, picking her teeth, scratching herself, stretching her fingers and holding her head contemplatively in her hands. Occasionally she twists herself around the branch and hangs by one of her long, hairy arms.

Next she climbs down a couple of thick aerial roots and begins what looks like a gentle morning workout, hanging by both arms, then by one arm and a foot, stretching, and swinging and tumbling about. Dessert follows—a few fistfuls of young, green liana leaves—before she swings steadily through the trees to her siesta in the shade. On the way she stops now and then for more fruit, and a drink of water, scooped from a hollow tree fork.

She is young and single. Like most of her species she lives alone and keeps herself to herself. Should she encounter other orangutans, even in the same fruit tree, she would scarcely acknowledge their presence. The orangutans of Borneo are not sociable animals, except during the mating season, when a couple will stay together for a few days. This is probably because there is not enough food to supply whole troops of them.

In the rainforest there are always some trees with abundant fruit, no matter the season. The animals and birds concentrate around them—monkeys, hornbills, parrots, fruit doves and multitudes of smaller birds. After dark, bats, slow lorises and other nocturnal creatures come out to feed.

Through the ages the orangutan has fascinated man because of its comical similarity to us—in appearance, facial expressions, patterns of movement and intelligence. Anyone who has seen a young orangutan is struck by its resemblance to a human baby. In its first three years, it is comparable in size, development and speed of learning. This engaging red ape is clearly one of mankind's closest relatives.

The orangutan is Malaysia's national animal, and much is being done to protect it. The greatest threat is its shrinking habitat—caused less by logging than by the intensive cultivation of crops that often follows in the wake of the lumbermen.

The ape can survive tree felling, but not total cultivation of the land. Poaching is another serious threat. As with other creatures, the orangutan's best hope of survival is the rapidly growing popular interest in wildlife and nature conservation in Malaysia and Indonesia.

The orangutan can grip as well with its feet as with its hands. It lives best in lowland rainforest and mangrove swamps. If visitors come too close, it may hurl large branches down from the trees.

Today the orangutan is found only on the islands of Borneo and Sumatra, but it used to live all over Southeast Asia and southern China. Hunting and the clearing of forests for agriculture rendered it extinct in those areas.

Description

Danum Valley—169 square miles (438 sq km) of mountain-, swamp- and lowland rainforest with huge trees (mainly of genera *Ficus* and *Dipterocarpus*)—is considered to have some of the most undisturbed rainforest in all of Sabah, and it is in a class of its own when it comes to the amounts of wildlife. Good chances of spotting wild orangutans (density of 1–2 animals/sq km). Mountainous and hilly country, which makes long hikes quite an ordeal. A 14-mile (22-km) trail up to Mount Danum (10,827 feet/3300 m) and back is estimated to take five days. The area's inaccessibility has always been its best protection.

Great parts are still virtually inaccessible, but around the Danum Field Centre is a system of organized trails. Danum Valley was originally scheduled for logging, but through devoted work from Malaysian and international conservationists, in combination with increasing incomes from eco-tourism, the area now seems to be temporarily saved. All the forest outside the reserve has already been cut down or is scheduled for logging.

Danum Field Centre was built in 1985 and is a scientific research station and nature education center. Malaysian and foreign researchers work here, primarily studying how different ways of logging affect fauna and flora. School classes from all over the country also come here to learn more about nature and conservation.

A bridge over the Segama River leads into the reserve. There are 19 miles (30 km) of marked trails, a 115-foot (35-m) high observation tower, a visitors' center with exhibitions and a nursery for economically interesting rainforest trees.

Fauna of interest

MAMMALS: Asian elephant, binturong, Bornean gibbon, Sumatran rhinoceros, banteng, clouded leopard, leopard cat, 10 species of monkey (among them, orangutan and proboscis monkey), western tarsier, bearded pig, sun bear, red giant flying squirrel.

BIRDS: 250 bird species, for instance, bat hawk, great argus, buffy fish-owl, 4 species of pitta, trogons, hornbills and several local passerines.

OTHER: Atlas moth (one of the world's largest moths).

Seasons

Open all year round. Warm (68–86°F/ 20–30°C) and humid. Cooler at higher altitudes. Main rainy season is during the northeast monsoon, from October to February, but it may rain at any time.

How to get there

International flight to Kota Kinabalu or Kuching. Domestic flight to Lahad Datu. Daily bus to the Danum Field Centre. Taxis available as well. In the area all movement is on foot. Local guide mandatory for longer hikes.

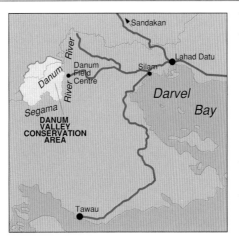

Permission needed for independent visits can be obtained from Yayasan Sabah/Sabah Foundation in Kota Kinabalu.

Accommodation/food/camping

A simple hostel at the research station. Bring your own food. More comfortable lodging is being built. Often full during weekends. Book through Yayasan Sabah/Sabah Foundation in Kota Kinabalu. There is a small hut on Mount Danum that can be booked in the Danum Field Centre.

Other areas

Taman Negara National Park, West Malaysia. Impressive lowland-rainforest area of 1,677 square miles (4343 sq km), one of the richest in wildlife in all Southeast Asia. Malayan tapir, tiger, sun bear, Sumatran rhinoceros, clouded leopard, gaur, Asian elephant, white-handed gibbon, great argus, 4 species of pittas, bat hawk, eagles, 7 species of kingfishers, 5 species of hornbills. Well-organized visitors' center at Kuala Tahan, 186 miles (300 km) northeast of Kuala Lumpur.

Good lodging, trails, guides.

November to February is the rainy season. Plenty of leeches.

Taman Kinabatangan and Gomantong Caves Game Reserve, Sabah, Malaysia. Comprising 162 square miles (420 sq km), along the lower reaches of the Kinabatangan and Sungai Menangol rivers, where the relatively undisturbed mangrove forest and lowland rainforest is interspersed with secondary forest, lakes and plantations of rattan and oil palms. The area is considered to have the greatest density of wild orangutans on Borneo. It also has nine species of monkeys, including the proboscis monkey (easiest seen during afternoons) and Bornean gibbon, as well as Asian elephant, saltwater crocodiles, Storm's stork (almost extinct), kingfishers and raptors. The Gomantong Caves system has millions of bats and swiftlets.

Khao Yai National Park, Thailand. With its 837 square miles (2168 sq km), it is one of the largest remaining continuous tropical forests on the Asian mainland. Altitudes between 656 and 4,265 feet (200 and 1300 m).

Tigers, Asian elephants, gaurs, sambars, Asiatic black bears, binturongs, white-handed gibbons. Also 300 species of birds, e.g., hill myna, hornbills and a range of local rainforest passerines. Easily accessible, 100 miles (160 km) from Bangkok, good trails, guides, food and lodging. Open all year round.

Ujung Kulon National Park, Java, Indonesia. Comprising 294 square miles (761 sq km). Javan rhinoceroses (45 out of a world total of 60!), leopards, bantengs, sambars, saltwater crocodiles, Java kingfishers.

Sepilok Forest Reserve and Orang-utan Rehabilitation Centre, Sabah, Malaysia. Comprising 171 square miles (443 sq km) of lowland rainforest, mangrove forest and secondary forest. Here orangutans that have been illegally caught and then confiscated by the authorities are rehabilitated to a life in the wild again. It is also a forest reserve with some 40 wild orangutans. The Sumatran rhinoceros is being reintroduced. School classes are educated in rainforest problems at the Nature Education Centre. Open all year round, 15 miles (24 km) from Sandakan.

Gunung Leuser National Park, Sumatra, Indonesia. Mountainous area of 3,861 square miles (10 000 sq km), with rainforests, rivers, wetlands and alpine vegetation (on Mount Leuser, 11,300 feet/3445m). One of Asia's largest national parks. Sumatran rhinoceros (200), orangutan and 6 other species of monkeys, Asian elephant, tiger, sun bear, Asiatic golden cat, leopard, clouded leopard, leopard cat, 320 bird species. Easily accessible at Gurah Recreation Forest, close to the Ketambe Research Station. Simple lodging and food, observation tower. The Bohorok Orang-utan Rehabilitation Centre lies within the park and works like Sepilok on Borneo. Simple lodging and good trails.

Tanjung Puting National Park, Kalimantan, Indonesia. 1,178 square miles (3050 sq km) of lowland rainforest on southern Borneo, with an orangutan rehabilitation center, run by the Canadian-Lithuanian researcher Biruté Galdikas. Species like in Danum Valley.

Tabin Wildlife Reserve, Sabah, Borneo, Malaysia. Comprising 473 square miles (1225 sq km) *Dipterocarpus*-rainforest. Orangutans common in the eastern part. Sumatran rhinoceroses.

Kulamba Wildlife Reserve, Sabah, Borneo, Malaysia. Comprising 80 square miles (207 sq km) swamp- and coastal forest. Perfect orangutan habitat with a large population of orangutans.

Tiger!
Bandhavgarh National Park,
Madhya Pradesh, Indien

The big male tiger spreads himself majestically on a hilltop, framed by an arch of bamboo leaves. A big, good-natured family cat with friendly eyes and a wise expression, his head on his paws—or so he appears at first sight. Seconds later, he fixes an ice-cold, predator's gaze on you, hisses viciously and looks ready to pounce.

Two camera-toting Indian tiger hunters suddenly feel like potential tiger food. The great cat is only 4 yards (4 m) away, and the woman in the blue sari sits with her husband seemingly unprotected on the excursion elephant. But they are safe so long as they stay on the back of their elephant. They are probably well aware that tigers kill some two hundred people a year in India but seldom, if ever, attack an adult elephant.

In the tiger's eyes the tourists are part of the elephant, a colorful outgrowth on its back. So you are quite safe riding on a trained one, and it will carry you in relative comfort through dense bamboo jungle.

Half an hour later the tiger gets up and pads away, flaunting the iron muscles under his elegantly striped

The Indian national parks of Bandhavgarh and Kanha offer excellent opportunities to view a tiger in the wild. Threats to the survival of this powerful cat increased with the marketing of "tiger-bone wine" used in Chinese folk medicine. This led to more poaching.

skin, setting his wide, heavy paws softly and silently. When he stands still, for a moment he melts into the background, his stripes matching the sharp, straight shadows cast by the bamboo stems, and his golden coat blending with the dry leaves. You could pass an arm's length away without spotting him. He lies down again a few hundred yards farther on, panting heavily in the heat. This allows the elephants to come fairly close, but 5 yards (5 m) seem to be the limit. Any closer and the tiger glares, hisses and shows his impressive teeth.

The mahout (elephant driver) gently urges his mount backward. For the tiger radiates authority and unlimited self-confidence. He is in command of his jungle. Five mahouts and their elephants have been tracking this cat since five o'clock in the morning. Every day they ride out in the pitch darkness before dawn to try to find some of the local tigers for the visi-

tors to see. By listening to warning calls from deer and langurs, reading spoor in the sand, interpreting the reactions of the elephants and the behavior of vultures and crows, they can work out where a tiger is to be found. And they know its favorite haunts.

They know, for example, that he won't be on a tree branch above them, ready to pounce down like a leopard. Unlike smaller cats, tigers seldom climb trees, although they will do so in an emergency. He could be in a river or a stream because—again unlike other cats—he doesn't mind the water and is a good swimmer.

The mahouts communicate from elephant to elephant by two-way radio, reporting the tigers' movements, and at the entrance to the national park visitors are told where to meet the mahouts. They are picked up along the forest road and board the elephants four at a time.

STEFAN WIDSTRAND

Tigers are threatened by trophy hunters, logging, population growth, and the increasing demand for tiger bones, used in Chinese folk medicine. The best hope for their future lies with the woman in the blue sari and the many other Indians who visit the tiger reserves every year. No one can avoid being impressed by the relaxed and at the same time explosive force of nature embodied in this magnificent animal. People who once have seen a wild tiger in its habitat will hopefully care more about its future.

Alert chital deer hinds (above) sniff for tiger scent in the air, and listen for warning calls from other animals. These relatives of European fallow deer are the tiger's favorite prey. Tigers hunt at night and in the early morning, particularly in summer when the days are terribly hot. They creep slowly up to their prey, then make a swift dash.

A young male tiger in the forest (previous two pages)

Description

The tiger has become the very symbol of the Indian conservation efforts. In 1973 the very ambitious Project Tiger was launched, with much support from the WWF. The numbers of Bengal tigers had dropped dramatically, from approximately 40,000 in the 1940s to a mere 1,800 in 1970. Tiger hunting was then banned, and impressive areas of virgin forest were set aside as national parks, reserves and buffer zones. Afterward the numbers of tigers increased, and within just a decade—according to official surveys—there were more than 4,000. But since then poaching has again increased noticeably, and furthermore many researchers believe that the results of these surveys have been exaggerated for political reasons. Several tiger reserves suffer from incompetent and corrupt leadership. Thus, in spite of the success of Project Tiger, there might still be as few tigers in India today as back in 1970. But this is nevertheless a major achievement.

Bandhavgarh National Park is today, together with the *Kanha National Park* and the *Ranthambos National Park*, the most reliable place in the world for spotting tigers in the wild. The area, previously a private hunting area for the Maharaja of Rewa, was declared a national park in 1968. It lies at 1,640 feet (500 m) altitude and covers 169 square miles (437 sq km), of which 40 square miles (105 sq km) is a core area and the rest a buffer zone. Eco-tourism here is better organized than in most other Indian national parks.

The country here is hilly and forested, mixed with open grass- and wetlands. The Bandhavgarh mountain (2,625 feet/800 m) dominates the surrounding landscape and it has an ancient fort and Hindu pilgrimage site on its top. The forests—mainly sal trees (*Shorea robusta*), bamboos and a range of fig trees—are more openly parklike, and the wildlife hence more easily observed than in other Indian national parks. Along river valleys and gulleys, the vegetation is lush and dense. The park is crossed by a web of jeep tracks, leading to all the important habitats. The ancient fort at the summit is still the private property of the Maharaja of Rewa and can be visited on foot, after special permission has been obtained.

Fauna of interest

MAMMALS: Bengal tiger, leopard, gaur (end of December to June), dhole (southern part), sambar, chital, Indian muntjac, wild boar, Hanuman langur, rhesus macaque, Indian gazelle (in the drier areas of the south), four-horned antelope, blackbuck (a few only).

BIRDS: Red jungle fowl, common peafowl, jungle owlet, crested serpent eagle, changeable hawk-eagle, Bonelli's eagle, Indian grey hornbill, Malabar grey hornbill, parakeets, white-shouldered ibis, vultures (e.g., black vulture) and local passerines.

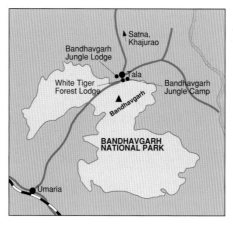

Seasons

The park closes completely during the monsoon, July 1 to October 31. November is the greenest month. December and January are cold. April onwards is baking hot. November and January/February are considered best for game viewing. Tigers can be seen throughout the open season, but count on spending several days in the park to have a fair chance of spotting one. Avoid weekends and Christmas, when the area is usually crowded. The park also closes during midday for the animals to rest.

How to get there

International flight to Delhi or Calcutta. Domestic flight to Khajurao, and then by local taxi for six hours (130 miles/210 km). Or take the train to Umaria and taxi from there one hour to Bandhavgarh. If one books in advance, the hotels arrange taxi-transfers from Umaria or Khajurao. The trip by car to Kanha National Park in the South takes nine hours.

Accommodation/food/camping

At Tala, outside the park entry gate, there are several hotels and lodges of varying standards and prices. *Bandhavgarh Jungle Camp* is an old colonial building, and the "rooms" are spacious tents. All the guides are professional biologists. *Bandhavgarh Jungle Lodge*, built as a small village, in local materials and style, is the best location. *White Tiger Forest Lodge* is the state-run hotel. Chalook Resort is small and personal. All hotels arrange jeep safaris in the park.

Other areas

Kanha National Park, Madhya Pradesh, India. With its 363 square miles (940 sq km), plus 388 square miles (1005 sq km) as a buffer zone, Kanha is one of the country's largest protected forest areas, and its probably most famous wildlife and tiger reserve. Here live 60–100 tigers, 50–60 leopards, gaur (700, in great herds and with huge males), dhole (100), barasingha (a special endemic subspecies found only here), chital, wild boar, nilgai, sloth bear, golden jackal, blackbuck (few), Hanuman langur, Indian muntjac, four-horned antelope. Kipling wrote *The Jungle Book* here.

Ranthambore National Park, Rajasthan, India. About 100 miles (160 km) from Jaipur. Until 1991 the classic tiger-watching place in India. But after some 20 tigers were poached here, during just one year, tiger observations here have turned rare. The park covers 154 square miles (400 sq km) and is still rich in other wildlife—nilgai, sloth bear, jungle cat, sambar, chital and leopard. Probably best from March to May, but also very hot then. Ranthambore is a fairly well-preserved wet-land and semi-desert ecosystem, set in the middle of an intensely cultivated and grazed landscape.

Gir Sanctuary and National Park, Gujarat, India. The last outpost for the once so common Asiatic lion. Some 250 of them live here, as do leopards, chitals, sambars, four-horned antelopes, nilgais and plenty of mugger crocodiles. Best from December to March.

Nagarahole/Bandipur/Mudumalai National Parks, Kerala/Karnataka/Tamil Nadu, India. Comprising 247/334/116 square miles (640/865/300 sq km). The finest complex of reserves in southern India, 62 miles (100 km) from Mysore. Probably the most important refuge for the Asian elephant (1,000+). Also tiger (best in Nagarahole), leopard, sambar, chital, Indian spotted chevrotain, Indian muntjac, wild boar, Indian porcupine, Hanuman langur, bonnet macaque, sloth bear, dhole, common otter. During the monsoon, Bandipur is best. February to May Nagarahole is best. Nagarahole is densely forested; Bandipur is more open.

Yala/Ruhuna National Park, Sri Lanka. With its 377 square miles (976 sq km), Sri Lanka's largest national park. Open October 15 to July 30. Asian elephant, leopard (Vepandeniya best), wild water buffalo, purple-faced leaf-monkey, sloth bear (May to June best), golden palm civet, mugger crocodile.

JAN PEDERSEN

Wings from All Asia
Keoladeo Ghana National Park, Rajasthan, India

It is a January afternoon on the Ganges plain. A wintering imperial eagle flies low over the acacia trees, causing a wild panic among thousands of waterfowl. Flocks of bar-headed and graylag geese rise with a deafening cackling and thunderous wingbeats. The trumpet notes of common cranes ring out, and masses of coots scuttle along the water, flapping furiously. Herons, storks, ibises, lapwings and cormorants scramble to safety. Oriental darters freeze and pretend to be part of the tree they are perched in, or disappear into the water.

When the eagle has passed, the water is still ruffled by the commotion. Down and small feathers fall, and the air vibrates from the wingbeats of the geese. The birds seem abashed, but thankful to have escaped once more.

If Keoladeo Ghana is a paradise for waterfowl, it is an Eldorado for raptors. In winter you can see ten species of eagles, and thousands of wheeling vultures. The water seethes with life—a living soup of frogs, toads, algae, water snakes, molluscs, leeches, marsh turtles, carp, water hyacinths, catfish, water beetles, duckweed, waterlilies, ciliates, water celery and plankton. This soup brings the waterfowl to the park. They feast on it and after that the eagles and vultures feast on them.

For hunters and hunted, it is a royal feasting place, and has been so since the days of the Queen-Empress Victoria and the British Raj in India. It was here that the fabulously rich Maharaja of Bharatpur established a tremendous duck-shoot for himself and his princely friends. By raising the water level, he created the wetlands that still attract ranging birds from as far away as Siberia and the Russian steppes. The princes killed thousands a day, but still the birds came to feast and winter.

With the British Empire gone from India and the maharaja's retreat, the slaughter of birds by humans has long since ended. The geese still come to what is now a national park, followed by eagles and vultures, but there is a new kind of audience, here to admire them.

In the cool twilight, when the day's spectacular bird show is over, a long line of pedal rickshaws heads back to Bharatpur. They carry not only foreign eco-tourists like us, but also ordinary Indian families who have spent the day picnicking in the park, watching the flocks through binoculars and consulting their bird books. Many of the rickshaw men are also know-ledgeable bird guides.

In the old days, the rickshaw men might have been hired as beaters or loaders of shotguns. Times have changed.

The Siberian white crane (opposite page) is one of the world's rarest birds. It breeds in Siberia and winters primarily in China, but some come to Keoladeo Ghana instead. Bar-headed geese (below) breed in the Tibetan highlands and migrate here from across the Himalayas.

The oriental tawny eagle (above) is closely related to the steppe eagle. More than thirteen species of eagle are found here in winter.

Most visitors to Keoladeo Ghana get to see the oriental darter (above) and the white-breasted kingfisher (right). The oriental darter has to dry its feathers after every dive because its plumage is not impregnated with grease like that of geese and ducks. The Indian python (below) is seldom seen, but helpful local boys will show you its holes.

Description

Keoladeo Ghana is a wetland area in the middle of Rajasthan, still world-famous for its teeming bird- and wildlife. In this hot and arid climate, fresh water is a scarce commodity, and the wetlands attract great numbers of birds and mammals, not only from nearby, but from many parts of Asia as well. Winter visitors here come from the distant tundra of Siberia, from the Mongolian mountains, the deserts of Kazakhstan and the steppes of Russia.

Approximately 12,000 pairs of herons, cormorants, storks and ibises breed here, and an additional 150,000 birds—mostly ducks, geese and coots—winter. Keoladeo has become famous also as the most easily accessible place in which to see the almost extinct Siberian white cranes. Some of these cranes winter in Keoladeo, but each year in lesser numbers. Soon they will probably be extinct.

This wet oasis was created for hunting purposes by the Maharaja of Bharatpur in the 1890s. He expanded the marshland area by raising the water level and swamping the surrounding lands. This action was successful in attracting waterfowl, who arrived in masses to breed and to winter, despite the grand yearly hunting parties that were held here for decades, with outright massacres of ducks and geese. Daily bags of several thousand birds were not uncommon, and the single-day record bag from 1938 was 4,273.

Keoladeo Ghana was declared a national park in 1981. Its very limited area (12 square miles/29 sq km) includes, apart from the lake and swamps, some surrounding arid bush savannah and gallery forest. These drier parts lie in the south, and that is the area to find deer, blackbuck and a range of semi-desert birds.

Large Indian pythons are common and can easily be pointed out by rickshaw drivers and nature guides. There is a good system of roads and trails, all for walking and biking only. The name "Keoladeo" derives from the name of the antique Shiva temple in the middle of the park.

Fauna of interest

MAMMALS: Nilgai (600), blackbuck, chital (650), sambar, rhesus macaque, wild boar, striped hyena, Indian porcupine, common palm civet, golden jackal, leopard cat, jungle cat, fishing cat, smooth-coated otter.

BIRDS: More than 350 bird species, e.g., painted stork (7,000 pairs), Asian open-billed stork (300 pairs), black-necked stork, spoonbill (100 pairs), woolly-necked stork, black-headed ibis (400 pairs), Sarus crane, Siberian white crane (very few, January to March), demoiselle crane, Indian darter, white pelican, Dalmatian pelican, greater flamingo, bar-headed goose, ruddy shelduck, Indian roller, 11 species of herons, 13 species of eagles (among them wintering imperial eagle, greater spotted eagle, lesser spotted eagle, Eurasian tawny eagle, steppe eagle, and breeding crested serpent eagle, Bonelli's eagle and

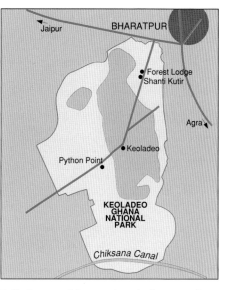

Pallas's sea eagle), 6 species of vultures, owls, kingfishers, bee-eaters, 16 species of ducks and 3 species of cormorants.

REPTILES: Indian python.

Seasons

The park is open all year round, but two seasons are best. One during the monsoon, when most of the 120 local bird species breed (August to October). The other during the winter (October to February), when the migrants from the north are here. Most migrants are in place January to February. Summers are hot (95–117°F/35–47°C, daytime) and very humid. Winters are cool (41–86°F/5–30°C, daytime; almost frost, nighttime).

How to get there

International flight to Delhi. Train, bus or taxi 112 miles (180 km) (4 hrs) to Bharatpur. Bicycles can be rented there for transport within the park. Or a rickshaw at the park entrance. The rickshaw drivers are, in many cases, excellent nature guides and they know all the best places for animals and birds. Having entered the center of the park, moving around on foot is easiest. An early-morning or late-evening punt trip in the marshland is recommended. Punt with skipper can be rented at the Shanti Kutir gate. Motor vehicles are not permitted.

Accommodation/food/camping

Anyone not wanting to rush around needs a couple of full days here. There are plenty of hotels and lodgings at all prices and standards in Bharatpur town. In the park itself are the comfortable *Forest Lodge* and the forestry department guesthouse *Shanti Kutir*, but these are often fully booked. Camping is not permitted.

Other areas

Chilka Lake, Orissa, India. The largest brackish-water lake in the country, situated at the coast, 100 miles (160 km) south from Bhubaneshwar. Probably the best bird area in India, with millions of migrants and hundreds of thousands of breeding shorebirds, herons, geese, ducks and storks. Best from December to February.

Qa el Azraq, Jordan. Wetland and desert reserve in the Jordan Desert, 68 miles (110 km) east of Amman. 38+32 square miles (100+600 sq km). Resting grounds for millions of passage migrants, especially March to May, but also September to November. Hundreds of thousands of ducks winter. Also striped hyena, mountain gazelle and Houbara bustard. Earlier there used to be cheetah, Arabian oryx, ostrich and Asiatic wild ass. Now they are to be reintroduced. One lodge. The area has dried out completely several times in recent years, due to increased fresh-water demand from the capital, Amman. The future of the reserve is uncertain.

Shiretoko Peninsula, Hokkaido, Japan. During winter, the greatest concentration anywhere of Steller's sea eagle (1,800 of the estimated world population of 6,000–7,000). December to March, but highest numbers in February. They leave their night roosts in the trees at Sashiruigawa at dawn and fly by the hundreds out toward the Nemuro Sound to fish. About 700 white-tailed sea eagles do the same.

Arasaki, Kagoshima, Kyushu, Japan. Thousands of cranes winter on former agricultural lands. November to February. Hooded crane (9,500), white-naped crane (2,400), demoiselle crane, Siberian white crane and common crane. Also white-tailed eagle.

Zhalong Nature Reserve, Heilongjiang, China. Comprising 162 square miles (420 sq km) grass- and wetland, one hour from Qiqihar. Easily accessible. Great numbers of waterfowl during the breeding season, e.g., Japanese crane, white-naped crane and demoiselle crane. Migrants are Siberian white crane, hooded crane and common crane. April to October.

Poyang Hu, Jiang Xi, China. A large lake, important as wintering ground for, among others, Siberian white cranes (up to 2,500, or 95 percent of the world population!), hooded cranes (750), white-naped cranes (2,000), swan geese, great bustards and oriental white storks. November to February.

Koko Nor, Qinghai, China. A lake of 19 square miles (50 sq km) at an altitude of 7,546 feet (2300 m) in the Tibetan high plateau. Spectacular landscape and high-altitude birds. Black-necked crane, Pallas's sea eagle, saker falcon, thousands of bar-headed geese and shorebirds. Hides available. May to September.

Mai Po, Hong Kong. Migration and wintering grounds for thousands of shorebirds, ducks, herons and raptors. Very easy access. September to May.

On Foot or Elephant among the Rhinos
Royal Chitwan National Park, Nepal

Before our hike in the park, our guide Bal Kumar lays down the rules:

"If we meet a tiger on the path, everyone must stop, stand still, be quiet and wait until it goes away. If we meet a sloth bear, we must all bunch together, wave our arms, clap our hands, make a great din and try to look big and dangerous. If we meet a rhino, everyone get ready to jump into the elephant grass or climb a tree. No one move unless the rhino attacks. It has poor eyesight and often runs forward a little just to see and recognize smells better."

As he makes these points to our group of international eco-tourists, some smile in anticipation, others wonder if they should go birdwatching instead.

"We are armed, so don't worry," says Bal Kumar, displaying a yard-long wooden stick. "This is very effective against rhinos."

"What if we're attacked by a tiger?" asks a tourist.

"Then we'll run as fast as you!" he grins.

He is a Tharu, a master at interpreting animal tracks and moving about silently in the wild. The Tharu tribe of hunters has lived here for centuries, and many who used to be poachers are now tourist guides. Pulses race when two Australians spot our first tiger tracks in the soft clay beside the path. Is the tiger lying in wait for us? "The tracks are at least three hours old," reports Bal Kumar. "It'll be several kilometers away by now. Maybe…"

An hour later, we find the first rhinoceros tracks through the elephant grass: deep, three-toed impressions of feet bearing an awesome weight. Bal Kumar checks that all his charges are together. Suddenly a massive great Indian rhinoceros lumbers along the trail, heading straight for us. Everyone comes to a dead stop—guide, tourists, rhino. Then everything happens very fast. The rhino snorts and rushes forward. The visitors throw themselves headlong into the elephant grass. Only Bal Kumar remains standing there, holding his stick in front of him. A yard away the colossus stops, snorts, then turns with astonishing agility and retreats at full tilt. Those who see it can hardly believe their eyes.

Why, one wonders, should a great Indian rhinoceros with a foot-long horn, be scared of a small man with a yard-long stick?

Obviously Bal Kumar knows, but it remains a mystery to the rest of us. Because of his bad eyesight, the rhino may not have seen us at all, only rushing towards us because he heard or smelled strangers.

Despite his immensely heavy hide, which fits in sections like armor-plate, but is thicker, he is fast and agile on his feet, and could stop and turn on a dime. Maybe he just wanted to scare us because he was in a bad mood, as rhinos sometimes appear to be. If this one just wanted to scare us, he certainly succeeded.

They have a reputation for bad temper and stupidity, yet their horns are said to have magical medical properties, which is one reason why they are still threatened by hunters.

On the afternoon visit to the rhinos, most of the group elect to go by elephant instead.

Riding on an elephant in tall elephant grass (above) is uncomfortable, but the only way to get through.

The great Indian rhinoceros (left and right) is threatened by poachers who are after its horn. Nearly a quarter of the world's remaining great Indian rhinoceroses live in Chitwan.

69

The chital deer (above) is one of the most common large mammals in the Indian and Nepalese forests. If there is plenty of game available, the tiger does not attack man or his cattle. Attacks come when people have shot all its natural prey or cut down its forest. Tigers known to be man-eaters have usually been wounded by hunters in the past. Tigers kill two hundred people a year in India, illustrating the problem of protecting dangerous animals. Wildlife wardens point out that several hundred thousand Indians are killed every year in traffic accidents. This tiger (left) is a young male.

Description

Royal Chitwan National Park is Nepal's first, created in 1973 in what was formerly royal hunting land, protected as such since the early 19th century. During British colonial times Chitwan was the setting for grand hunting parties, with thousands of beaters and hundreds of elephants. Bag totals for one single hunting party could number up to 120 tigers, 38 rhinos and 27 leopards! During the 1950s and 1960s the reserve was under heavy poaching pressure. The wild water buffalo was then exterminated, as was the Barasingha deer. The great Indian rhinoceros decreased in numbers, from about 2,000 to 100. From 1973 onwards, though, poaching has been virtually unheard of, after the Royal Nepalese Army Gurkha soldiers began guarding the park boundaries. Today the numbers of rhino have increased to around 350, and Chitwan thus holds about a quarter of the world population of the species. The authorities have also started to transfer rhinos from here to other reserves and national parks in the country, to reintroduce the species to areas where it formerly existed.

Chitwan lies in the lowlands of Nepal, the Terai, consisting of the open flood plains around the Narine and Rupti rivers, and a low mountain ridge, the Churia Hills. The higher parts are covered by tropical moist forest, with the sal tree (*Shorea robusta*) as the dominant species. The wet plains are covered by high elephant grass and riverine gallery forests. The biggest population (about 150) in the world of a threatened crocodile species, the gharial, lives in the part of the Narine running through Chitwan. At the park headquarters in Kasara Durbar, there is a breeding station, where they, with support from the WWF, raise young gharials for reintroduction, here and in other places along the Ganges water system. The threatened Ganges dolphin also lives in this part of the Narine.

One of the most important ecological factors in Chitwan is the annual grass harvest, carried out by people from the surrounding areas during December and January, and the ensuing burning of the stubble. This centuries-old practice is mainly responsible for keeping the land relatively open and rich in wildlife today. The grass then grows more quickly during the spring, which strongly favors the grazing game. It is also much easier for visitors to see the animals. The grassland is dotted with several marshes and small lakes. Lake Devi Tal is a favorite haunt for rhinos and mugger crocodiles. Chitwan is also a good area for spotting sloth bears. The best areas for wildlife observation in the park are around Tiger Tops/Devi Tal and around Chitwan Jungle Lodge.

Fauna of interest

MAMMALS: Great Indian rhinoceros (350), Asian elephant, Ganges dolphin, tiger (about 60), leopard, jungle cat, fishing cat, leopard cat, gaur (best from February to April), sloth bear, hog deer, chital, sambar, Indian muntjac, wild boar, Hanuman langur, rhesus macaque, dhole, smooth-coated otter.

BIRDS: 490 bird species, e.g., common peafowl, red jungle fowl, great Indian hornbill, lesser adjutant stork, black-necked stork, 13 species of herons, woolly-necked stork, gray-headed fishing eagle, crested serpent eagle, Bengal florican, vultures, ducks, geese, shorebirds.

REPTILES: Gharial, mugger crocodile, Indian python, monitor lizards.

Seasons

Monsoon climate with high humidity, at its driest April to May. December to February are cool, the rest of the year (especially May to September) is hot. The rains begin in May/June and end in September. After the monsoon the land is green and the skies are often crystal clear, with the peaks of the Himalayas fully in view on the northern horizon, some 62 miles (100 km) away. In the wintertime there is often fog, up to 10:00 A.M.

The plains are burnt off in January/February. Thanks to this, it is much easier to see the animals from February to May than in the autumn. To see 20 rhinos on a spring day is not uncommon. Crocodiles are easiest to observe in October to February, when they lie along the river shores, basking in the sun. The best season for birds is February/March, when wintering, migrating and breeding birds are in place. In June/July, Chitwan is practically inaccessible due to the rains.

How to get there

International flight to Katmandu. Domestic flight to Meghauli, close to the park or bus (5 hrs, 103 miles/165 km) via Tandi Bazaar to Chitwan. There is also the option of a two- or three-day river-rafting ride down the Trisuli/Narine. All serious travel agencies in Katmandu can organize transport and book lodging. Many tours available. In the park one can walk, go by jeep, be paddled in a canoe or ride an elephant. There are also some observation towers where one can spend the night. The large lodges have their own elephants, and the government has an elephant station at Sauraha.

Accommodation/food/camping

Lodging and food from budget to luxury. Budget alternatives are all outside the park, most of them at Sauraha, and it can be difficult to reach the best areas from there. Of the more expensive options, some lie within the park: legendary *Tiger Tops Jungle Lodge* which, together with the *Chitwan Jungle Lodge*, lies in the finest part of the park. *Tiger Tops Tented Camp* lies on the island of Bandorjhula in the Narayani. *Elephant Camp* and *Gainda Wildlife Camp* are at Sauraha.

Other areas

Royal Bardia Wildlife Reserve, Nepal. Comprising 374 square miles (968 sq km). Species and habitats like in Chitwan, plus barasingha, nilgai and blackbuck. Good chances for tiger. Here they are now reintroducing rhinos from Chitwan. Good from November to May, best from February to April.

Sagarmatha National Park, Nepal. Comprising 480 square miles (1243 sq km) of high alpine country around the world's highest mountain, Sagarmatha (or Mt. Everest). Glaciers, barren rocky fields, moors, rhododendron forests and pine/spruce forests. Himalayan tahr, common goral, mainland serow, alpine musk deer, Asiatic black bear, red panda, blood pheasant, Himalayan monal pheasant, lammergeier, Himalayan griffon and other high-altitude bird species. Best from October to May.

Corbett National Park, Uttar Pradesh, India. Comprising 317 square miles (820 sq km). Mammal species as in Chitwan, plenty of wild elephants but no rhinos. Good chances of seeing tigers. 580 species of birds. Open November to June. Best February to May. The "core area" around Dhikala is richest in wildlife.

Kaziranga National Park, Assam, India. Often considered as India's finest national park. Comprising 166 square miles (430 sq km) of open grassland with patches of forest. The great Indian rhinoceros has increased here to about 1,000, meaning that Kaziranga holds more than 60 percent of the world population of the species. Also tiger, leopard, leopard cat, wild water buffalo, Asian elephant (herds of 200–300), Asiatic black bear, capped leaf monkey, Hoolock gibbon, barasingha, hog deer, Pallas's sea eagle and various species of pheasants. Best from November to March. Tourism is well organized.

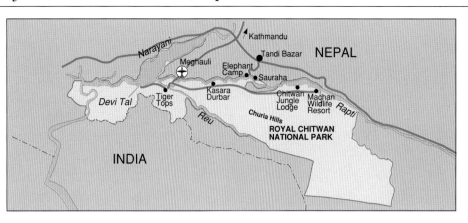

A Paradise for Crocodiles and Birds
Kakadu National Park, Northern Territory, Australia

When Johnny Banjo bent down to drink from the river, he had no idea that he would soon be famous. In a flash, an enormous crocodile shot out of the muddy water, clamped its jaws around his head and dragged him down to the bottom of the river. Crocodiles drown their victims before dismembering and eating them.

Luckily for Johnny, an Aborigine, his arms were still free. He pressed his thumbs into the crocodile's eyes, its weak spot, as hard as he could, and it relaxed its grip just enough for him to wriggle free and escape. Next day a picture of Johnny Banjo with his head swathed in bandages was splashed across the front pages of all major Australian dailies.

The incident highlights the problem of protecting dangerous animals. By no means all crocodiles are dangerous to humans, but the big estuarines certainly are.

MAGNUS ELANDER

In northern Australia, an average of one person a year is killed by them, and others are injured, usually when bathing. Legislation protecting crocodiles was keenly debated before being passed in the 1970s.

The South Alligator River flows through Kakadu National Park, where we step into a small flat-bottomed aluminum boat belonging to Rob Lee, a local guide, for a trip into crocodile territory. Rob has lost his left leg, but denies that a crocodile took it.

Scenes in the film *Crocodile Dundee* were shot here. The water is muddy and you can't see what's down below. Its flow is swift, and in the wrong direction—from the coast inland—because of its tides.

We go upstream, to a bend in the river that is the crocodiles' favorite haunt. Between tides, this becomes mud, and we have to turn back well before the river dries up again.

Soon we have crocodiles all around us. They surface right beside the boat. Sometimes only a pair of nostrils and a pair of eyes appear; sometimes a rough, scaly back. Lazily moving their tails, they accompany us for a while, then vanish below the surface.

"That's Big Yellow," whispers Lee. It is his pet name for a ferocious-looking light-colored crocodile nearly 20 feet (6 m) long. "He's the biggest one we now have on the river, but you used to find 10-metre (32-foot) brutes."

He shuts off the engine and lets the current take us in to the graphite-gray mudbank where the creatures are sunbathing. Annoyed by our presence, Big Yellow raises himself up until he is half-standing. His bent, "moon-lander" legs stick out from his sides and seem to have difficulty holding up his long body. Crocodiles can't stand completely upright. When on land they usually move at a slow crawl, dragging their tails behind them, but when they get excited they can run at good speed, with the body held well off the ground, easily outrunning any human.

When he has grown tired of staring at us he takes a few rotatory steps and disappears beneath our boat.

The estaurine crocodiles used to be common throughout Southeast Asia and Australia. They have long been hunted and killed for their valuable hides, used in making shoes and handbags, and to adorn leather. After the Second World War, the hunting became so extensive that they were threatened with extinction.

Today, this feared and persecuted creature at last has been given a refuge in the sparsely populated north of Australia.

MAGNUS ELANDER

On a boat trip on the Yellow Water, near Cooinda, you meet much of the wildlife of Kakadu—the estuarine crocodile (opposite page), large flocks of pied geese (above), Australian pelicans (below), little pied cormorants (right) and many other wetland birds.

MAGNUS ELANDER

SVEN HALLING

At dusk great flocks of squawking white cockatoos—the picture above shows a little corella cockatoo—arrive on their way to their roosting trees, while the estuarine crocodiles (below) hope for a good catch when nocturnal animals come down to the riverbanks to drink.

Description

Kakadu National Park is located in the northern, tropical part of Australia's Northern Territory, a good 124 miles (200 km) east of Darwin along Arnhem Highway. It covers 6,757 square miles (17 500 sq km). The park consists mainly of flat and low-lying dry eucalyptus forests that gradually change into savannah and grass plains. The Alligator River area consists of sedge-grown wetlands, swamp forests and permanent open-water ponds, so-called billabongs. The eroded mountains of Arnhem Land to the east and south have pockets of monsoon rainforests, scenic canyons, streams and cascades. Kakadu is unique because most of the major habitat types of Australia's "Top End" are found there. The paved highway to the visitors' center in Jabiru was completed in connection with the opening of one of the world's largest uranium mines there in the 1970s. The park is managed by Aborigines in cooperation with the National Parks and Wildlife Service.

Kakadu is famous for its crocodiles. There are two species—the estuarine crocodile and the freshwater crocodile. Fully grown estuarine crocodiles sometimes attack large prey, including man, while the freshwater crocodile is regarded as less harmful. It is, however, not always easy to distinguish between the two species.

The park authorities have some simple but important rules to prevent attacks by crocodiles when exploring Kakadu and other equivalent places in northern Australia. It is recommended that tents be put up no closer than 55 yards (50 m) from waterways, that you never climb branches or logs overhanging deep pools, that you keep arms and legs inside boat hulls and that you never bathe or swim in potential crocodile waters.

About 200 species of birds nest and have their home in Kakadu. Another 100 are visiting migrants from the northern hemisphere or southern Australia. The water buffalo was introduced 150 years ago, and reproduced rapidly and uncontrolled. Through a determined management program, the population is now kept to roughly 10,000 head, compared with an earlier maximum of 60,000. Wild feral pigs are another problem that needs to be handled.

Fauna of interest

MAMMALS: Dingo, water buffalo, feral pig (running wild), several smaller marsupials, sugar glider, rock ringtail possum, 8 species of kangaroos (kangaroos, wallabies, rock wallabies, and wallaroos), dugong.

BIRDS: Emu, Australian pelican, Australian darter, 12 species of herons, black-necked stork, 3 species of ibises, royal spoonbill, magpie goose, whistling-ducks, Radjah shelduck, green pygmy-goose, Brahminy kite, whistling kite, white-breasted sea-eagle, peregrine falcon, brown falcon, brolga, comb-

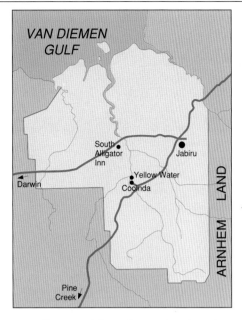

crested jacana, rainbow pitta, waders, 4 species of cockatoos, lorokeets, 7 species of kingfishers, rainbow bee-eater, 17 species of honeyeater, great bowerbird.

REPTILES: Estuarine crocodile, freshwater crocodile, lace monitor (tree goanna).

Seasons

All year. Best is the dry season, i.e., May to September, with daily highs at 86°F (30°C) and low humidity. During the rainy season, November to March, high humidity in combination with temperatures of 95°F (35°C) may be uncomfortable. Night lows are rarely below 77°F (25°C). Some roads are impassable during the rainy season and others require four-wheel-drive vehicles all year round. Estuarine crocodiles display particularly aggressive behavior during the mating season, October to April.

How to get there

International air service to Darwin, Northern Territory, and onwards by bus, 2 1/2 hours to Cooinda or South Alligator in Kakadu. Guided tours start in Darwin, where also rental cars

and camper-vans are available. Guided nature trips can be booked at the hotels in the park or at any tourist bureau. Crocodile watching from boats along South Alligator River is booked in Kakadu Holiday Village, and birding boat trips in Yellow Water are booked at Four Seasons Cooinda Hotel. Aerial sightseeing is arranged regularly from the airstrip in Jabiru. Hiking trails through various habitats are kept open, and information regarding these is available at the visitors' center in Jabiru.

Accommodation/food/camping

Three hotels in the national park, at Cooinda, Jabiru and South Alligator. Youth hostel at Border Store. Campsites at several places in the park as well as camper-van parking. *Muirella Park* and *Nourlangie Creek* are the nicest. Restaurants and stores are found at or near the hotels.

Other areas

Lakefield National Park, Queensland, Australia, 2,074 square miles (5370 sq km), is the most accessible park on the Cape York peninsula. Open savannah-like grassland with a sparse eucalyptus forest along the extensive floodplains. Pockets of gallery forest. Estuarine crocodiles and freshwater crocodiles are common, several species of kangaroos, e.g., eastern grey kangaroos, dingos (wild dogs), feral pigs and lots of birds in lakes and wetlands, e.g., magpie goose, brolga, black-necked stork, several species of cockatoos. Completely impassable December to March due to the precipitation. Four-wheel-drive vehicles mandatory April to November. Campsites.

Iron Range National Park, Queensland, Australia. Tropical lowland rainforest on the east coast of the Cape York peninsula. Spotted cuscus, grey cuscus, common striped possum, cassowary, palm cockatoo, Eclectus parrot, estuarine crocodile. One-quarter of Australia's butterflies, including one of the largest species in the world, the atlas moth. Accessible by four-wheel-drive vehicles from Cairns (except December to March, due to rains) or by small aircraft. Campsite.

Most crocodile attacks occur when people are bathing.

MAGNUS ELANDER

Kangaroos and Koalas
Wilson's Promontory National Park, Victoria, Australia

Torrential rain spatters the eucalyptus trees. It is winter here in the south of Australia. Two eastern grey kangaroos peer out from between the tree trunks. At first glance they look like deer, for only their heads are visible in the tall grass. For a while, they stand motionless, ears up and eyes alert.

Suddenly they bound away, revealing that they are Australia's national symbol. Using their tails for steering and balance, they cover the ground with giant two-legged hops. They are the size of full-grown men, and each jump would win them any open athletics championship. A dozen others now materialize and join the fleeing pair.

Rainfall is irregular in many parts of Australia. If grazing land dries out, the kangaroos decline in number, but they recover astonishingly quickly when the land turns green again. After several years of drought in the early 1980s, the number of large kangaroos fell from about 19 to 13 million. After a few good years, they were back to their original level.

Thanks to its pouch, the kangaroo is perfectly adapted to a capricious environment. A marsupial can have three young at the same time in different stages of development: one almost fully grown that has left the pouch; another living in the pouch; and a fertilized egg ready in the womb. The egg starts to develop as soon as the pouch is empty. When the older one leaves the pouch for good, a new baby is born. The female mates again immediately, and another fertilized egg is in position.

In the evening the sun gleams between blue-gray clouds and casts sharp-edged shadows on the light-colored sandy ground. Kangaroos appear from all directions, becoming more active as the day draws to a

MAGNUS ELANDER

close. In an opening among the trees, a female grazes beside an almost fully grown youngster.

The mother is literally sitting on her tail. The kangaroo's tail is a valuable all-purpose appendage, more important than the tails of other large animals, which mainly use them for flicking at flies. It is long and very heavy. Like a tightrope walker's pole, it provides balance when the big body is airborne between hops. When the kangaroo is walking slowly with its forefeet on the ground, the tail and forefeet provide support while its big, flat hind feet move forward, and when the entire animal is sitting upright, it acts as a prop.

A flock of sulfur-crested cockatoos flies squawking out of a treetop, causing the kangaroos to prick up their ears. They could have been startled by dingoes, the Australian wild dogs, on their evening hunt. The young kangaroo feels insecure, hops to its mother and tries to hide its head in her pouch. Soon it has squeezed its whole body in there. Somehow it succeeds in folding its long hind legs and powerful tail into a compact package. The pouch is now at bursting point—but the youngster manages to turn around and stick its head out.

The female tries a few jumps, as if to shake everything down into place, and seems unbothered by her front-heavy load. When she bends forward to graze, the one in the pouch can reach the ground and do the same. It is safe and secure, sheltered from perils and the fickle July weather.

There are about fifty species of kangaroos in Australia. The eastern grey kangaroo (above and opposite page) is as tall as a full-grown man and weighs nearly 200 pounds (90 kg). The smallest is littler than a rabbit and weighs barely 1 pound (500 g).

In Wilson's Promontory, people are wakened by the noisy laughing call of the kookaburra (below), also called the "laughing kingfisher."

SVEN HALLING

After the African ostrich, the emu (below) is the world's largest bird. It is nomadic and will walk long distances to rainy places. Sex roles are reversed, and the male sits on the eggs, going without food for eight weeks at a time. The koala (bottom) lives on the succulent leaves of the eucalyptus, which provide both nourishment and moisture. "Koala" is an Aborigine word meaning "does not drink."

The common brushtail possum (top) comes down from the treetops at night when enticed by honey or other goodies. Crimson rosellas (above) are happy to both drink and bathe when the opportunity arises.

Description

Wilson's Promontory National Park covers 189 square miles (490 sq km) of the most southeasterly peninsula on the Australian mainland, 143 miles (230 km) southeast of Melbourne. The bedrock is granite and the landscape is mainly arid. The highest peak is Mount Latrobe, at 2,474 feet (754 m). Four different habitats can be distinguished.

Extensive tidal shores are exposed at low tide along Corner Inlet, a bay which is bordered by saltmarshes and mangroves. During the austral summer, up to 50,000 waders winter here, most of them migrants from eastern Siberia.

Open grasslands, changing into heath toward the south, are characteristic of Yanakie Isthmus, the narrow neck of land connecting Wilson's Promontory to the mainland. In several places there are smaller stretches of wetlands as well as areas with very dense vegetation. Eastern grey kangaroos and emus are abundant, and kangaroo congregations numbering several hundred animals are not unusual.

The promontory proper is a rocky peninsula. A devastating forest fire ravaged it about 50 years ago, and therefore the present vegetation is dense and impassable, except along cleared roads and trails. Tall eucalyptus grooves cover the mountain slopes. There are also pockets of temperate rainforest with extensive stands of tree ferns and swamp gum. Koalas are fairly common among the tall eucalyptus along the Lilly Pilly Gully nature trail, 1,640 yards (1500 m) north of Tidal River.

The coastal strip extending 80 miles (130 km) along the Promontory has nice sand-duned but rather unproductive beaches. Occasionally a white-breasted sea-eagle is seen here. On the islands off the coast, little penguins, common diving-petrels and short-tailed shearwaters nest. A permit is required to land. Tongue, Pillar and Norman points are excellent spots for viewing pelagic birds like the wandering albatross and the Australian gannet.

Fauna of interest

MAMMALS: Eastern grey kangaroo, wallabies, koala, common wombat, common ringtail possum, echidna.

BIRDS: Wedge-tailed eagle, brown falcon, white-breasted sea-eagle, 21 species of waders (several Siberian migrants), herons, straw-necked ibis, black swan, emu, sulphur-crested cockatoo, crimson rosella, rainbow lorikeet, ground parrot, laughing kookaburra, Cape Barren goose, little penguin, albatrosses, short-tailed shearwater, common diving-petrel, Australian gannet. More than 250 different bird species are observed.

Seasons

Good all year but quietest during the cool months of the austral winter, when somewhat fewer visitors come to this otherwise extremely popular national park.

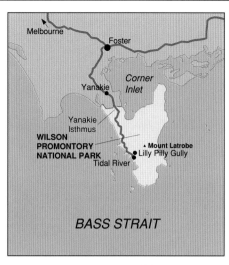

BASS STRAIT

How to get there

International air service to Melbourne, and then by car via Foster and Yanakie to Tidal River, the main settlement in the park. From there 50 miles (80 km) of trails take visitors through all the habitats in the park, either solo hiking or as part of guided weekend hikes. Maps and trail guides are available in the information center at Tidal River, as is information on wildlife and nature. For those with limited time, day trips are available from Melbourne.

Accommodation/food/camping

Plain hotel and sleeping cabins at Tidal River, as well as an extensive camp or camper-van site. General store and coffee-shop. Along the trails there are some 10 smaller campsites with various degrees of comfort. Pre-booking is necessary. Camping elsewhere in the park requires a permit, easily obtainable from the park office in Tidal River. When the park is fully booked, there is accommodation in Fish Creek and Foster, outside the park, and there are campsites at Yanakie and Waratah Bay.

Other areas

Wyperfeld National Park, Victoria, Australia, 386 square miles (1000 sq km) in the arid plains 249 miles (400 km) northwest of Melbourne, preserves a stretch of the Mallee in its original state. Eastern grey kangaroos and emus are common. Parrots, particularly sulphur-crested cockatoos, galahs and Mallee ringneck parrots, abound, and a soaring wedge-tailed eagle is a common sight. Mallee fowl nest in the park.

Phillip Island, Victoria, Australia, 40 square miles (101 sq km), is an island 75 miles (120 km) southeast of Melbourne with thousands of nesting little penguins, more than half a million short-tailed shearwaters, 5,000 Australian fur seals and several koala sanctuaries. One of Australia's best wildlife areas. At Summerland Beach the "Penguin Parade" attracts about a hundred thousand spectators each year to watch the little penguins emerging from the sea a few minutes after sunset every day. The western spit is a good lookout point for pelagic birds like the wandering albatross, the Australian gannet and the giant petrel.

Lamington National Park, Queensland, Australia. Comprising 78 square miles (202 sq km) of subtropical mountain rainforest, where the most prominent peaks reach up to 3,600 feet (1100 m). The park is located 72 miles (115 km) from Brisbane and houses not only a great variety of birds, including lyrebirds (tallest passerine in the world), Australian brush turkeys, bowerbirds, green catbirds, king parrots and galahs, but also nocturnal marsupials like the red-necked pademelon, common brushtail possum, common ringtail possum and suger glider. Two lodges, *O'Reilly* and *Binna Burra*. Campsites.

Eungella National Park, Queensland, Australia, 196 square miles (496 sq km), tropical and subtropical rainforest in the Clarke Ranges, 50 miles (80 km) west of Mackay. Kangaroos, greater gliders, suger gliders, echidnas, bandicoots. Main attraction is the platypus, easily spotted near the campsite at Broken River. Only camp and camper-van sites.

Mission Beach, Queensland, Australia, 82 miles (132 km) south of Cairns, is the most reliable place to see the cassowary, the large ostrich of the rainforests. Most rewarding is a slow hike in the early morning along trails and dirt roads in the rainforest a few miles from the coast. Motel and youth hostel.

Wau, Papua New Guinea. The mountain rainforests surrounding Mount Kaindi, 7,956 feet (2425 m), are the home of a dozen different birds of paradise. A minor road up the mountain, negotiable only by four-wheel-drive vehicles, offers great opportunities to watch not only birds, but also the long-nosed echidna, gliders and tree-kangaroos. Simple accommodation in Wau and at the Wau Ecology Institute. Wau has an airstrip served by small aircraft from Port Moresby.

Despite warning signs, many kangaroos become traffic victims.

On the Continent of Penguins and Ice
The Antarctic Peninsula, Antarctica

Antarctica is the world's coldest and windiest continent, with the least precipitation. It can drop to -130°F (-90°C) here, and winter gales blow at nearly 190 miles per hour (300 km/h) over thousands of miles of continuous inland ice. Nearly everything about this southernmost continent is contradictory. Only 2 percent of its surface is ice-free, even though it receives less precipitation than the Sahara. And yet, during the southern summer, Antarctica literally explodes with life—in the water, in the air and on land.

The reason is the wealth of food in the surrounding seas. Most important is the krill, a shrimp-like creature not quite 2 inches (5 cm) long, which is found in vast concentrations of several million tons. It provides a rich spread for fish, cuttlefish, seals, and a whole range of birds, as well as the great baleen whales.

At Pauleton, we find a million Adélie penguins occupied in raising the next generation. When the Zodiac boats ferry us ashore, we are met by a host of these birds, totally unafraid. Tightly packed, they stand bickering and chattering in a huge colony on the ice-free slopes. Above them, brown skuas and kelp

while the young males practice territorial battles in the sea nearby. The stony beaches are full of chinstrap penguins, and Cape petrels soar around the higher hills. In the approach to Gerlache Strait, the water is full of krill and it is not long before the surface is broken by blowing humpback whales. Sometimes schools of killer whales pass between the icebergs. Crab-eater seals lie on nearly every ice floe, and from time to time a penguin-eating leopard seal appears. Like other sea-birds, penguins are fond of resting on the sculptured ice that, in a variety of shapes, floats in endless succession in all the channels, in ever-changing conditions of light and weather.

It was the animal life that first drew man to the ice-filled and inhospitable waters of Antarctica, and it is still the wildlife that today attracts visitors here from all corners of the world. Whales, seals and penguins used to be slaughtered for economic gain in the form of meat and oil. Now tourists pay to see and experience the almost unbelievable numbers of animals and birds. On the ships, there are knowledgeable guides who not only provide information about what the eye registers and the mind wonders at, but also see to it that the rules for eco-touring are adhered to: take nothing except photographs; leave nothing except footprints.

Antarctica is not a no-man's land, nor does it belong to any single nation. Friends of the environment all around the world have therefore pointed out the possibility of making the whole continent into a supranational park—a world park, in fact. The Antarctic environment continues to be cleaner and more untouched than anywhere else on earth. Its wildlife is immensely rich, and supremely worthy of protection.

Adélie penguins (above left) and Weddell seals (below) are common along the coasts of Antarctica.

gulls hover, and snowy sheathbills run between the nests. All three species are trying to grab an egg or a penguin chick. Antarctica has no terrestrial carnivores. Cape petrels from nests on the high cliffs of Deception Island follow our ship in great swirling flocks, often accompanied by Antarctic fulmars and ponderously gliding giant petrels. Wilson's storm petrels dart about above the surface, and on the beaches or floating ice floes we pass Weddell seals in deep sleep. Now and again young fur seals appear—surprisingly, since at one time they had virtually been killed off.

Around Elephant Island, the sea swell is so strong that it is impossible to go ashore. With the aid of binoculars, however, it is easy to pick out elephant seals on the shore. They doze there during the fur-shedding season,

STEFAN LUNDGREN

With a wingspan of up to 12 feet (3.5 m), the wandering albatross (right) commands the stormy waters of Drake Passage between South America and the Antarctic Peninsula. The southern continent has no terrestrial carnivores, but in the surrounding seas there are both killer whales (above) and leopard seals (below), which specialize in catching penguins.

Standing 3 feet (1 m) tall, the emperor penguin (previous page) is the world's biggest species of penguin. This one is in the eastern Antarctic.

Description

Antarctica is larger than Europe and is covered by the largest area of inland ice on earth—with a thickness of up to 13,125 feet (4000 m). The Southern Ocean is also a part of the Antarctic ecosystem and its extension toward the Atlantic, the Indian and the Pacific oceans is limited by a border zone called "the Convergence."

East Antarctica lies on primary rock and is not easily accessible. Tourist expeditions operate only occasionally in this part of the continent. The immensely long, icy coast is visited by only a few scientific expeditions each year. East Antarctica is the breeding territory for most of the colonies of emperor penguins, among other species.

West Antarctica is largely of volcanic origin and is actually an archipelago connected by the inland ice. The Antarctic Peninsula is the largest and northernmost of these islands, and also the most accessible part of Antarctica. The west coast and its islands have a maritime climate that is fairly stable during the austral summer. Early mornings may be foggy, but as the sun breaks through, temperatures often climb well above the freezing point. Intermittent spells of rain, hail and snow occasionally turn into blizzards.

The landscape in West Antarctica is dominated by ice and snow, but during the austral summer the most extensive snow-free coastal areas on the whole continent may be found here. Impressive mountain peaks protrude through the glacial ice and can be steep where they descend straight into the sea. The flora is extremely sparse, while the fauna consists of very few species but large numbers of each: penguins, pelagic birds, seals and whales. The only strictly terrestrial bird is the sheathbill. Among the places at which the tourist ships usually call, the following may be mentioned:

Elephant Island. Regularly pounded by heavy swell that often prevents safe landings. Elephant seals, fur seals and Weddell seals share the shoreline with nesting chinstrap penguins. Thousands of Cape petrels in the mountains; the only place to find macaroni penguins in the Antarctic.

Esperanza, with the Argentinian station on the northern tip of the Antarctic Peninsula, has a colony of Adélie penguins (100,000 birds).

Paulet Island, a small volcanic island, has a colony of Adélie penguins numbering more than 1 million birds.

Fildes Peninsula, on King George Island in the South Shetland archipelago, is the largest ice-free area in the Antarctic, at 10 square miles (25 sq km). Here research stations from nine different countries, a post office and a gift shop crowd together, influencing the wildlife negatively. The remainder of a chinstrap penguin colony is found on the island of Ardley.

Deception Island. A majestic volcanic island (latest eruption 1969) with a channel large

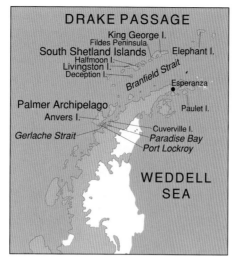

enough to permit even big cruise ships to pass all the way into the crater. Beside an abandoned Norwegian whaling station, there are hundreds of nesting Cape petrels and a minor colony of chinstrap penguins.

Halfmoon Island, sheltered by Livingston Island in the South Shetland archipelago, has one of the largest colonies of chinstrap penguins, and on the easternmost cape there are smaller numbers of Antarctic shag.

Yankee Harbour, near Halfmoon Island, is a former American whaling station, nowadays with a sparse colony of gentoo penguins. Farther south, at the northern inlet of Gerlache Strait in the Palmer archipelago, is *Two Hummock Island*, with waters rich in krill. The best area to see humpback whales. Farther into Gerlache Strait is *Cuverville Island*, with gentoo penguins on the beach ridges, kelp gulls in the cliffs and a large inaccessible colony of brown skuas. Breeding gentoo penguins and Antarctic shags at *Paradise Bay* and *Port Lockroy*. Plenty of brown skuas and sheathbills.

Fauna of interest

Drake Passage
BIRDS: Wandering albatross, black-browed albatross, gray-headed albatross, yellow-nosed albatross, sooty albatross, light-mantled sooty albatross, storm petrel, brown skua, petrels, diving petrels, shearwaters, terns.
Antarctic Peninsula
BIRDS: Adélie penguin, gentoo penguin, chinstrap penguin (10 million), southern and northern giant petrels, Antarctic fulmar, snow petrel, kelp gull, Wilson's storm petrel, Antarctic shag, brown skua, Antarctic skua, Antarctic tern, Arctic tern, snowy sheathbill.
MAMMALS: Weddell seal, crab-eater seal (the world's most numerous seal), southern elephant seal, leopard seal, Antarctic fur seal, humpback whale, minke whale, killer whale, sei whale, fin whale (occasionally).

Seasons

Austral summer (end November to February), the only season when Antarctica is accessible

by ship (tourism, with few exceptions, is by ship). Best wildlife viewing in December and January. Weather is variable but relatively stable during the austral summer.

How to get there

International air service to Punta Arenas in southern Chile or Ushuaia in southern Argentina. Ushuaia is the gateway to Antarctica, and the majority of expedition and cruise ships depart and arrive here. Most visitors have pre-booked their cruise, but today there is also a decent chance to find stand-by tickets in Ushuaia. During the cruises passengers are taken ashore at selected places by rubber dinghies to get a close view of the wildlife. From Punta Arenas, there is an air service to a Chilean transit airport at Fildes Peninsula on King George Island, giving tourists access to various parts of Antarctica by air. A few sailing boats organize private expeditions to West Antarctica. A few cruise ships make the last trip of the season a more extensive one by including East Antarctica and ending in New Zealand. So far, the 1990s have seen an average of 5,000 to 8,000 tourists per year in the Antarctic.

Accommodation/food/camping

All accommodation and all meals are on board the cruise ships. Research stations belonging to different nations provide the only permanent housing on the whole continent. The American McMurdo Base is renowned. The only hotel on the continent is a Chilean transit hotel on King George Island, to serve airborne tourists and scientists.

Other areas

South Georgia, United Kingdom, an isolated 124-mile (200-km)-long sub-antarctic island, mountainous and dissected by fjords, was until the 1960s an infamous large-scale whaling center some 1,865 miles (3000 km) east of Tierra del Fuego. Nowadays the island is the place to go to among the sub-antarctic islands to see penguins, albatrosses and whales. Millions of macaroni penguins, 200,000 gentoo penguins, 100,000 king penguins, 300,000 elephant seals, 1 million Antarctic fur seals.

Falkland Islands, United Kingdom. A cluster of islands in the South Atlantic 310 miles (500 km) east of Patagonia in Argentina, famous for its penguins and seals. King penguins (Volunteer Beach), rockhopper and macaroni penguins (Kidney Island), Magellan, rockhopper and gentoo penguins, South American sea lion and Antarctic fur seal (New Island), southern elephant seal (Sea Lion Island). Hotel in Port Stanley and local lodges. Well-organized tourism through Falkland Islands Tourist Board.

Condors, Rheas and Guanacos
Parque Nacional Torres del Paine, Chile

STAFFAN WIDSTRAND

South America's most famous bird glides over and slowly circles, intent on two hikers on the ground below. The Andean condor is a symbol of strength and power, an allegory of Andean history, myth and legend. This one is a male, with a fine, reddish-purple cock's comb, a beautiful white collar, a large white patch on the upper wing; the rest of his plumage is a sooty black. He is nearly 10 feet (3 m) from wingtip to wingtip and weighs 24 pounds (11 kg)—the world's largest bird of prey. It is easy to see why he is the central figure in the old tales Andean Indians tell their children.

The lake is grayish-blue and full of light-blue icebergs, for it is summer and at its far end the Grey Glacier is calving little bergs. Behind looms the 9,843-foot (3000-m) summit of the Paine Grande and the towerlike formations of the Cuernos del Paine.

Sunlight flicks on and off, directed by the passing clouds, whose curtains close, then are drawn back. Thirty condors wheel beside a sheer rock face. Maybe they have spotted a dead or dying guanaco or maybe they just fly together for the pure fun of it. Once up on a morning thermal current, they fly for mile after mile in search of food.

They are living sailplanes. Naturalist Charles Darwin observed one in flight for half an hour without seeing one flap its wings. They are comfortable at elevations of up to 16,000 feet (5000 m), where their remarkable flying skill is used to best advantage.

It has taken them a long time to learn it. A condor is one year old before it can fly at all.

Being vultures, they only feed on carrion, attracted to areas with large numbers of sheep, goats and deer as well as guanaco, vicuña, sea lions and seabird colonies.

They are said to be able to exist without food for more than forty days, but when they find it they gorge themselves.

They used to be a common sight in the Andes, but no more. Now they are rare, partly because of persecution by man, partly because the guanaco and

STAFFAN WIDSTRAND

STAFFAN WIDSTRAND

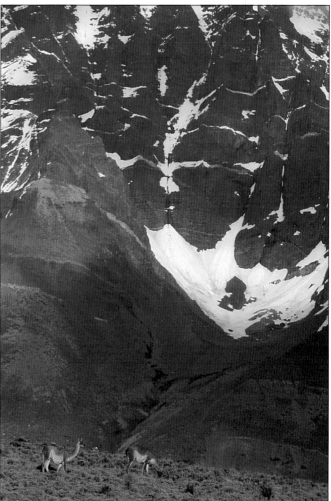

STAFFAN WIDSTRAND

A male condor (opposite page) climbs in the morning sun.

In the Torres del Paine massif (top), the Andean condor is still common, thanks to the abundance of game, particularly guanacos (above and right). These are the original wild llama, and one of the few animals that can live off the sparse grass here.

vicuña have been hunted to extinction. Only in the southern parts of Chile and Argentina do they survive in strength, along with the guanacos.

The hills here are rife with guanacos, posing on ridges, against the sky. A small flock clusters near our track. Mothers with camel-like eyes and long lashes suckle their babies, while a young pair chase each other in a complicated love dance. They take little notice of us, because this is not a hunting area. Elsewhere, they are extremely timid.

The scrub country here is typical of the Andes. Its climate is extreme, its pastures meager. The guanaco, a wild ancestor of the llama, is well adapted to wind-torn land. It copes far better than the livestock introduced by man, for the hardiest sheep find it hard to survive here. Millions of guanacos, and the closely related vicuñas, used to live on the deserted steppes of South America. They were killed off because land-owners feared they would compete with the sheep for the grazing, and South Americans lost a valuable economic resource, for the vicuña's wool is the most valuable in the world. It is remarkably long, fine, soft and lustrous. It has always been expensive, and now it's even more so, because there are so few vicuñas left in the wild.

Perhaps one day we'll see vicuña steaks, cutlets and

The Andean condor is the world's biggest bird of prey, weighing nearly 24 pounds (11 kg), with a wingspan of more than 10 feet (3 m). It is now common only in the southerly parts of the Andes, in Chile and Argentina.

wool in the more exclusive shops, all garnered in a sustainable way from the windswept wastes of South America.

In the evening, a more common animal emerges. Someone throws a bag of garbage into the rubbish bin at the campsite and is met by a sudden stench. It comes from a black-and-white striped skunk foraging in the bin, displeased at receiving a knock on the head from a trash bag. The smell lingers a long time. A passing fox wrinkles its nose and changes direction.

Three gray bushes suddenly rise from the ground and reveal themselves as lesser rheas and run off, zigzagging at speed. After them, like carriages in a toy train set, scoot thirty chicks. The male lesser rhea looks after the eggs and chicks. Many females will lay their eggs in one male's nest.

Description

Parque Nacional Torres del Paine lies in the Andes, in Región de Magallanes on the southern tip of Chile, just at the edge of the Great Patagonian Ice-Field, Campo de Hielo Sur (at 7,723 square miles [20 000 sq km] the world's largest area of inland ice after Antarctica and Greenland). The heart of the area is the four impressive and graphically elegant mountain massifs: Cuernos del Paine, Torres del Paine, Almirante Nieto and Paine Grande—all world-famous among rock climbers. With peaks between 8,530 and 9,843 feet (2600 and 3000 m), it is not the altitude above sea level that is the main attraction, but the dramatic and brutal beauty with which they rise from the surrounding plains.

There are many habitats here—semi-desertlike wastelands, grass plains, lush forests of false beech, steep mountains, Patagonian steppes, meandering rivers, ponds, soda lakes, flowering meadows and glaciers calving shining blue icebergs into cold lakes.

At the end of the 19th century the first settlers arrived to these areas, driving off the natives and starting cattle ranching on a grand scale. Forests were cut or burned down and the grasslands were heavily grazed. All predators were remorseless hunted and the edible game was seen as grazing competitors and killed off.

Parts of the park were set aside as a reserve in 1959. The protected areas were then enlarged step by step, and in 1970 Parque Nacional Torres del Paine was created. In 1979 and in 1993 its area was increased, and it now covers some 965 square miles (2500 sq km).

Mountain hiking and outdoor life have become very popular in southern South America in recent years, and during the austral summer (November to February) there are many backpacking and camping Argentineans and Chileans around. There is a good system of trails, and the rangers at the entrances to the park are very helpful and knowledgeable.

Since the park was founded, the wildlife has recovered rapidly and is now an example of what can be achieved if one wants to restore the faunal splendor of the past. Torres del Paine is one of the places in South America were one can be most sure of spotting Andean condors, lesser rheas and guanacos. Pumas are seen here more regularly than almost anywhere. The best wildlife areas of the park are along its eastern parts, both inside and outside the border. Practically tame foxes are often seen around the entrance gates in the east.

Fauna of interest

MAMMALS: Puma, guanaco (3,500), Chilean huemul, Patagonian mara, Patagonian skunk, Culpeo fox, Argentine grey fox.
BIRDS: Andean condor (up to 40 breeding pairs, up to 40 birds often seen together), black-chested buzzard-eagle, crested caracara, chimango caracara, short-eared owl, austral parakeet, ashy-headed goose, upland goose, peregrine falcon, Magellanic woodpecker, Chilean flicker, great horned owl (in the trees of

the park HQ/visitors' center), ferruginous pygmy owl, lesser rhea (300), southern lapwing, buff-necked ibis, torrent duck, flying steamer-duck, spectacled duck, lake duck, black-necked swan, Coscoroba swan, Chilean flamingo, great grebe, silvery grebe and Magellanic oyster-catcher.

Seasons

The wildlife is more interesting and the area easier to visit during the austral summer, November to February. The weather varies several times daily—there is almost always sun somewhere. The mountains are often visible early in the morning and are covered by clouds by noon/afternoon. Clearest weather is in the austral autumn, March/April. The Patagonian wind blows all year round and summertime temperatures are around 50–68°F (10–20°C).

How to get there

International flight to Santiago in Chile. Domestic flight via Puerto Montt and Punta Arenas, and then bus to Puerto Natales, Chile. Or Argentinean flight/bus to Rio Gallegos or Porvenir, and bus from there to Puerto Natales. It is also possible to reach Puerto Natales via a three-day boat cruise from Puerto Montt, through the wild and uninhabited fjord archipelago of southern Chile. A new road is being built from Calafate in Argentina to Torres del Paine and Puerto Natales.

Daily bus excursions are arranged from Puerto Natales, riding the dirt road 106 miles (170 km) to Torres del Paine and returning either the same day (boring, shaking and stressful) or another day. Maps can be bought and cars rented in Puerto Natales, for those wanting to see more, stop in many places and be mobile. The park is huge, distances are great and there are several interesting areas along the road leading there.

Accommodation/food/camping

The hotel *Hostería Pehoe* lies on an island in the Lago Pehoe. *Posada Río Serrano* is more rustic old-style and lies near the park headquarters at Lago Toro. There is a grocery shop with camping food. Four public campsites are

available, the one at Lago Pehoe being the most comfortable. As long as proper care is taken, camping is allowed anywhere in the park. There are ten *refugios*, simple multibed cabins. Riding- and packhorses can be hired at the park headquarters, where there is a visitors' center/museum.

Other areas

Parque Nacional los Glaciares, Argentina, is similar to Torres del Paine. The FitzRoy mountains are just as popular among alpinists and the area is just as good for hiking. The glaciers on the Argentinian side are much larger, but the area is less rich in wildlife: guanaco, Andean condor (common), buff-necked ibis, torrent duck, austral parakeet, sheld geese, black-chested buzzard-eagle, lesser rhea. Some small lakes here hold the rare hooded grebe, first discovered only in 1974. Calafate is the best starting point. Reached by bus from Rio Gallegos. Best from December to March.

Parque Nacional Tierra del Fuego, Argentina, lies in the Tierra del Fuego, on the border to Chile. The country here reminds one of the coasts of Norway or New Zealand. The richest biological zone of the park is the seashore and the Beagle Chanal. South American sea lion, South American fur seal and whales. Many pelagic birds as well—cormorants, skuas, shearwaters, petrels, gulls, albatrosses, sheld geese, steamer-ducks and penguins. Inland can be seen the black-chested buzzard-eagle, Andean condor, Magellanic woodpecker, austral parakeet and a range of local passerines. Easily reached from Ushuaia with daily buses. Several boat trips on the Beagle Canal organized daily from Ushuaia.

Halfway between Puerto Natales and Torres del Paine, several Andean condors spend their mornings hanging in the wind. They can be viewed at close range here.

STAFFAN WIDSTRAND

The Guano Islands of the Incas
Reserva Nacional Parácas and Islas Ballestas and Chincha, Peru

"Lobos marinos!" cries Johanna Jiborn-Gonzalez, a delighted four-year-old. Sea lions!

The crossing from the mainland has been boring, but now it's all worthwhile. The boat is tossing in the waves under the cliffs, but this does not bother her. With saucer eyes, Johanna watches hundreds of the big lobos romp on their private beach.

Hefty males fight until blood runs. They fling themselves at each other, bite necks, roar and bellow. Each defends his little strip of beach. In the heat of the battle, the females noisily protect their whimpering babies from being crushed by the struggling bodies. Some are newly born, and their placentas still lie on the sand, to the delight of the big Peruvian gulls. Johanna is absorbed by the action.

"Look, Mom, the little one is being squashed …

and look, that big one is getting chewed!" The Pacific breakers crash on the beach and splash foaming over *los lobos marinos*, the "sea wolves," as they are called in Spanish.

The air above is full of seabirds—Peruvian boobies, Peruvian pelicans and Guanay cormorants. On Ballestas and Chincha, dry, stony islands off the coast of Peru, there are millions of breeding pairs. The islands are so covered with their droppings they look like icebergs.

This bird manure, or guano, as the Incas called it, has been collected here for centuries, traded and used as a nitrogen-rich fertilizer over wide regions of the Andes. The Incas distributed it throughout their empire, which based its power on well-developed agriculture and a smoothly running infrastructure. Guano from Ballestas, Chincha and the other islands was a cornerstone of their economy.

90

Peruvian pelicans (above) and Peruvian boobies (below) are found in large numbers on the coasts of Peru and Chile. On the mainland, they breed on cliffs, but on the islands, they prefer level ground. So the guano, their droppings, is easy to collect for fertilizer. Sea lions (opposite page) lie packed like sardines on their beaches.

In 1810, Peru began exporting it, and by mid-nineteenth century a yearly harvest of some 50,000 tons of it was being scraped off the rocks and shipped out. Farmers loved it because it was richer in fertilizing value than seal guano or bat droppings from caves. To maintain the supply, the government still protects the seabirds, who consume 1,000 tons of fish a day in order to produce it.

Johanna finds the sea lions much more fun. And the pelicans which fish near the boat. On the return trip she watches 20,000 Peruvian boobies put on a display of nosediving into the sea. They plummet into a dense shoal of fish, each bird aimed seaward like a spike. When they hit the water, thousands of little fountains spurt. Johanna's eyes are wide once more. Then, exhausted, she falls asleep in her father's arms.

She will talk about the sea lions for a long time to come.

Guano is still collected today on the Ballestas islands (above). But since the 1960s, there are fewer birds to produce it—a result of overfishing by man. The elegant red-legged cormorant (left) is found only along the Peruvian, or Humboldt, Current.

Description

The Parácas peninsula reaches out like a hammer into the Pacific Ocean from the otherwise practically straight Peruvian coastline. A little farther out lie the Ballestas and the Chincha Islands. This part of Peru is mainly desert and semi-desert, with hot days and cool nights. On land there is almost no animal or plant life, hardly even grass. All living beings here—humans, animals, birds and plants—live from what the ocean gives, and the ocean gives quite a lot. The cold Humboldt Current comes up from the Southern Ocean, bringing water rich in nutrients from the depths up to the ocean surface along the coasts of Chile and Peru.

Warm and cold waters meet, making life conditions perfect for one of the most numerous species of fish in the world—the anchoveta. This small herring-like creature, since decades back, has given Peru the status of being the world's number one fishing nation. It also provides the biological base for a marine birdlife with few equivalents in the world. On the Peruvian coast and on its islands there are colonies with several million breeding pelagic birds. Before man succeeded in overfishing these waters during the 1960s, some 18–20 million pairs bred here; nowadays there are no more than 2–6 million. If the anchoveta disappears, so does the life conditions for all birdlife here, for the sea lions and for man.

Nearly all these islands, including the Ballestas and Chincha, are owned by PescaPeru, the government-run fishing company, which is in charge of both the fishing and the guano industry of the area. Parácas, though, is a nature reserve and no guano is harvested here.

The best observation points on the peninsula are the steep cliffs of Punta el Arquillo, the fishing harbor at Lagunillas and the muddy beach of Bahía de Parácas. Parácas is also a good place to see Andean condor. One pair breeds regularly, and often a few additional individuals spend some time of the year here. They usually prefer hanging in the winds over the steep cliffs above the sea-lion rookeries.

Fauna of interest

MAMMALS: South American sea lion (Ballestas and Punta el Arquillo), South American fur seal, whales (several species), dolphins (several species), Argentine grey fox.

BIRDS: Humboldt penguin, great grebe, Inca tern, Andean condor (best February to April), turkey vulture, Guanay cormorant, red-legged cormorant, Peruvian booby, Peruvian pelican, American skimmer, Peruvian tern, band-tailed gull, Chilean flamingo, peregrine falcon, skuas, petrels, shearwaters, storm-petrels, albatrosses, frigatebirds and North American shorebirds.

REPTILES: Marine turtles of several species.

Seasons

Strong winds can blow all year round, worst in June to August, but before 10:00 A.M. it is usu-

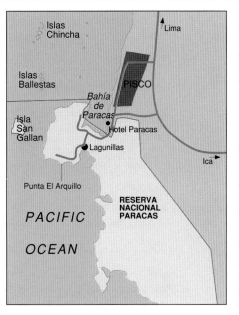

ally very calm. November/December is the main breeding season for most of the bird species. The sea lions give birth to their young in January/February. February to April is best for condors. June to August have largest numbers of flamingos. July to September is the "Garúa" season, with fog or haze and overcast skies in the morning. Very little rain.

How to get there

International flight to Lima. Rented car or bus 149 miles (240 km) south on the Panamericana highway to Parácas/Pisco. Ballestas and Chincha Islands can be visited by boat, but to go ashore special permission from the head office of PescaPeru in Lima is needed. Boat trips are arranged by the Hotel Parácas or by fishermen from the village of Parácas. A cruise to the Ballestas and back takes about five hours, and to the Chincha a full day. It is best to be out there early. Around 8:30 A.M. all the hundreds of thousands of Guanay cormorants take off from their nests almost simultaneously, and then fly together to their common fishing grounds. On the Parácas Peninsula, one needs a car for transport.

Accommodation/food/camping

Camping in the reserve is allowed but not recommended. One has to bring everything. *Hotel Parácas* is a luxury beachfront hotel. Several *pensions* and simpler hotels are available in the fishing town of Pisco.

Similar and nearby areas

Islas Mazorca, Peru, lies outside Huacho, 62 miles (100 km) north of Lima, and are another group of guano islands, with species similar to those as in Ballestas/Chincha, but in even greater numbers. Permission to go ashore is necessary.

Colca Gorge, Peru, lies a half-day's drive northwest of the city of Arequipa. Crúz del Cóndor is a viewpoint here, a very good

lookout point from which to see Andean condors at close range. They spend the night on the steep walls of the gorge, and then fly out around 8:00 A.M., passing very close to the lookout. The road up to Colca leads through desert as well as wet Altiplano moorland with a range of very interesting wildlife. Here lies the *Refugio de Patahuasi*, a WWF reserve, with great numbers of vicuñas, guanacos, Culpeo foxes, mountain viscachas, Andean geese and an array of local high-altitude bird species.

Laguna Salinas, Peru, is a large salt lake, located east of Refugio de Patahuasi, holding an interesting array of bird species, e.g., Andean avocet, three species of flamingos and several very local species.

Parque Nacional Machalilla, Ecuador. 212 square miles (550 sq km) of sandy beaches, coastal cliffs, bushland, dry forests and coastal rainforest near Santa Elena on the coast northwest of Guayaquil. Tamanduas, sloths, several species of monkey, brown pelicans, frigatebirds, blue-footed boobies, marine turtles. In Santa Elena there is a large area of saltpans with masses of shorebirds, flamingos of two species, herons and gulls.

Reserva Ecológica Manglares Churute, Ecuador. 135 square miles (350 sq km) of mangrove forest, tidal mudflats and lagoons southeast from Guayaquil. Jaguar, ocelot, puma, red howler, roseate spoonbill, horned screamer, woodpeckers, herons and wintering North American shorebirds.

Parque Nacional Podocarpus, Ecuador. 564 square miles (1462 sq km) of mountainous country, with páramo moorland, cloud forest and lush forests of elsewhere almost extinct *Podocarpus* trees. Entrance via Loja and Vilcabamba. Open all year. Good trail system. Puma, spectacled bear, white-tailed deer, fasciated tiger heron, torrent duck, Andean cock-of-the-rock, quetzals, trogons, tanagers, hummingbirds, parrots, guans, mountain toucans and several very local bird species.

Sea turtles may soon disappear from this area. People who buy these souvenirs are contributing to their extinction.

STAFFAN WIDSTRAND

The Richest Amazonian Rainforests
Reserva de la Biósfera del Manu, Peru

From Cuzco, once the capital of the Inca kingdom, a narrow road runs against a backdrop of snow-covered mountains through Andean villages largely unchanged since Pizarro conquered them in the sixteenth century. The road climbs over a 13,000-foot (4000-m) mountain pass, to reach the *páramo* plains.

From the lookout point at Tres Cruces, we see the entire Amazon basin spread out below us. A thick, green carpet stretches as far as we can see—the biggest rainforest in the world. It was a source of Inca splendor—gold, ornamental feathers and rich harvests.

The Manu Biosphere Reserve is a huge, but little-known wildlife area. Its 3.7 million acres (1.5 million ha) shelter 15,000 plant, 1,000 bird and 200 mammal species, plus several million types of insects. We arrive by four-wheel-drive truck, carefully negotiating a steep winding track. The upper reaches of the forest are wreathed in perpetual clouds, and rain falls every few hours.

moss, lichen, ferns, orchids, bromeliads and climbers. In two hours we identify a hundred species of birds. They flaunt bright colors—emerald-green quetzals and trogons, red and green parrots and parakeets, bright orange Andean cock-of-the-rocks, purple jays, rainbow-colored tanagers, hummingbirds and finches. The hummingbirds hover thickly around the flowering plants of the cloud forest.

We spend the night in a simple lodge by a rushing stream, where we see white-capped dippers, Andean cock-of-the rocks, spectacled bears, nightjars, owls, and colorful frogs, then continue downhill into a warmer climate, with taller trees and even more diverse flora and fauna.

A full day's trip in a fast outboard-powered canoe takes us down the temperamental Alto Madre de Diós River to the Manu River, which meanders through the lowland rainforest, and which we then follow upstream, leaving the last signs of civilization well behind. For mile after mile we pass through truly virgin tropical rainforest—a rarity these days.

Caimans bask on sandbanks along the river; huge screaming macaws fly above us, and we encounter small troops of fearless monkeys—all sure signs that this area has scarcely been touched by man. Even the red howler monkeys are so fearless that they inspect us at close range. Black spider monkeys, brown capuchins, common squirrel monkeys and comical emperor tamarins abound. In eight days we see nine different species of monkeys.

Basking Terekay turtles are stacked like dominoes on logs in the water. (Locally they are considered a delicacy and those outside the reserve are rapidly being killed off.) Kingfishers streak past us, herons stand completely still to avoid being seen, and cormorants sit drying their wings.

Manu is one the best places in South America to see the elusive tapir and jaguar. Both are plentiful here, and their tracks abound, but we weren't lucky enough to see them. Local guides tell us the jaguar is seen once in about seven trips, and the tapir once in ten.

We camp in comfortable modern tents on a beach by a rainforest lagoon. We try fishing for catfish and piranha, which is permitted here. We hike along forest trails, make night trips by flashlight and paddle dugout canoes in the lagoons among the caimans and the hoatzins.

One, then two, and three curious heads break the surface. They whistle to each other, dive and resurface, each time closer to the dugouts. This is the giant otter, over 6.5 feet (2 m) long. Hunted close to extinction for its fine skin, it is safe here, and relatively tame, swimming right up to the boat.

This idyll on the reserve may last only as long as eco-tourism brings in revenue. Otherwise, oil drilling, logging, ruthless hunting and slash-and-burn farming will take over.

The red howler monkey (right), popular prey for hunters because of its excellent meat, is normally extremely shy; in Manu, it is quite fearless and very curious.

There are many brightly colored birds in Manu, but they're not easy to find. One of the easiest to spot is the yellow-rumped cacique (below right).

The hoatzin (below) is a primitive species, with a sort of claw on each wing like archaeopteryx, the very first bird.

STAFFAN WIDSTRAND

Making a tremendous din, colorful parrots (opposite page) try to gather enough courage to land on the exposed riverbank. The largest is the bright red, almost-3-feet (1-m)-long red-and-green macaw (top). Parrots for miles around gather here to eat the mineral-rich clay. Only after the big, green mealy Amazons land (bottom) do the macaws follow suit. Although threatened by the international trade in them, these may survive because of eco-tourism.

The giant otter (above) is one of the international attractions of Manu. It's worth more alive than dead because eco-tourism provides jobs for guides, cooks, boat drivers, lodge personnel and traders. Flaco (right with a newly caught piranha) works as a kitchen boy. He is learning to be a cook and a boatman. The piranha is common to the Amazonian waterways and not as dangerous as reputed.

STAFFAN WIDSTRAND

97

Description

Reserva de la Biósfera del Manu, created in 1973, covers more than 7,105 square miles (18 400 sq km) and is probably the South American rainforest region that is richest in numbers of species and in the amount of wild-life. It is one of the world's foremost natural reserves and, unfortunately, one of the least known. The region is visited normally by fewer than 200 people a year. Most of it is covered by lowland rainforest along the Manu and Alto Madre de Diós rivers, but the reserve extends also through a number of different ecological zones: up the slopes of the Andes, through the cloud forests, and finally up to the bare Andean moorland—the *páramo*. Along the Manu River lie a number of very interesting oxbow lakes, or *cochas*, all very rich in wildlife. Among the best of them are Cocha Salvador, Cocha Cashu, Cocha Otorongo and Cocha Gallareta. The national park itself is what is called a strict nature reserve, to which access is granted only to researchers with special permission. This immense region is inhabited by no more than a few hundred natives, from at least three different forest tribes. Most probably there is a fourth tribe, but up to now its members have avoided contact with the modern world.

Adjacent to the national park is an *"Eco-tourism Zone"* of 965 square miles (2500 sq km), where visitors may camp and experience the magnificence of the Manu under controlled conditions. Its forests are at least as rich in wildlife as any inside the park.

In addition, there is a buffer zone of 348 square miles (900 sq km), a so-called *culture zone* where some hunting, local forestry and agriculture may be carried on. Here, the WWF runs projects for the local people to learn how to exploit the flora and fauna of the rainforest more ecologically, using "agro-forestry" methods. These three zones together form the Manu Biosphere Reserve.

Fauna of interest

Lowland rainforest
MAMMALS: Jaguar, puma, ocelot, margay cat, capybara, 13 species of monkeys (including red howler, black spider monkey, squirrel monkey, brown capuchin, white-fronted capuchin, dusky titi monkey, common woolly monkey and emperor tamarin), South American giant otter, neotropic river otter, collared peccary, agouti, giant anteater, southern tamandua, sloths, Brazilian tapir, several species of opossums, tayra, and more than 100 species of bats.

BIRDS: Over 1,000 species of bird have been recorded, among them the king vulture, 7 species of macaws, over 20 other species of parrots, hoactzin, American darter, Jabiru stork, roseate spoonbill, Orinoco goose, green ibis, American skimmer, harpy eagle, Muskovy duck, spectacled owl, several species of toucans, guans, trogons, curassows, chachalacas, tinamous, and others. Several endemic species have been discovered here.

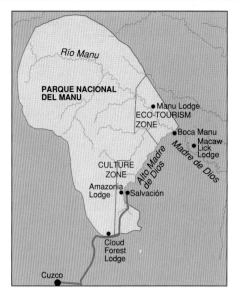

REPTILES AND AMPHIBIANS: Black caiman, spectacled caiman, bushmaster, fer-de-lance, common boa, anaconda, yellow-spotted side-neck turtle.

Cloud forests and páramo
MAMMALS: Spectacled bear, white-tailed deer, culpeo fox, puma, skunks.

BIRDS: Several hundred species, including Andean condor, Andean cock-of-the-rock, torrent duck, quetzals, trogons, humming-birds, eagles, tanagers and antbirds.
Rich in orchids and ferns.

Seasons

All times of year, but the local tour operators recommend the drier season, April to December. The driest time, and the best for spotting wildlife, is May to November: river and lake levels are lower, more land-dwelling mammals and caimans can be seen, and it is easier to camp.

How to get there

International flight to Lima. Domestic flight to Cuzco. Except for pure scientific expeditions, all visits to Manu must be arranged through one of the eco-tourism operators in Cuzco. Several of them are excellent and employ competent local biologists as guides.

The most interesting way down into Manu is by road. This takes a whole day by jeep/bus to Salvación, and then a further full day by motor canoe to Boca Manu. Otherwise you can take a light plane from Cuzco to the Boca Manu landing strip (45 minutes), where you will be met by the tour operator; this is much more expensive.

From Manu, a day by boat down the Madre de Diós River to Puerto Maldonado (20,000 inhabitants). From there, there is a scheduled flight to Lima or Cuzco. Yellow-fever vaccination is required for visitors to Manu.

Accommodation/food/camping

Cloud Forest Lodge lies on the route down to Manu at about 8,200 feet (2500 m), in the middle of the best parts of the cloud forest. *Amazonia Lodge* lies on the Alto Madre de Diós River, opposite the community of Salvación. Within a mile of the lodge, 510 species of birds have so far been observed, making it one of the places in the world where a record number of bird species has been counted. *Manu Lodge* is the only lodge in the Manu Eco-tourism Zone. It has a couple of observation platforms in high trees in the forest. *Manu Parrot Inn* lies close to a *collpa*—a mineral-salt lick—where the greatest number of parrots in the area gather daily. It lies outside the reserve proper, and the owners have therefore bought up all the surrounding land to establish a private reserve to protect the parrots. Basic lodging. The owner is a true bird expert.

Other areas

Zona Reservada de Tambopata-Candamo, Peru, comprises 5,710 square miles (14 790 sq km) of relatively undisturbed lowland rainforest and secondary forest south of Puerto Maldonado. In addition to jaguars, giant otters, and caimans, 572 bird species have been observed, among them the harpy eagle. The most important parrot lick in Peru is here, with daily gatherings of hundreds of macaws and thousands of other parrots. Other good sites are Lago Tres Chimbadas and Coco Cocha. Open all year. Lodging at *Tambopata Jungle Lodge*, *Tambopata Macaw Lick Camp* or *Explorers' Inn* (which is widely known in ornithological circles as a world-record site for the highest number of species observed (rivaled only by *Amazonia Lodge* in Manu). Camping trips can be arranged by Tabopata Nature Tours in Cuzco.

Santuario Nacional de Heath Pampas, Bolivia, with 3,900 square miles (10 110 sq km) protected rainforest, borders on the Zona Reservada de Tambopata-Candamo.

Mazaruni River, Guyana. Huge tracts of virtually untouched lowland rainforest with its fauna intact, especially upstream from Marshall Falls. Probably one of the world's best areas for spotting jaguars and Brazilian tapirs. In addition, sloths, collared peccaries, giant otter, capybaras, red howlers, spectacled caimans, fers-de-lance, bushmasters, coral snakes, scarlet macaws, king vultures, Everglade kites and toucans. Rainy season December to February, with high water levels. Mammals and caimans are easiest seen in the dry season, especially April to July. *Rainbow Safari Camp* is a basic camp at Marshall Falls. Others are being built upstream.

Air safaris all over the country are arranged from Georgetown.

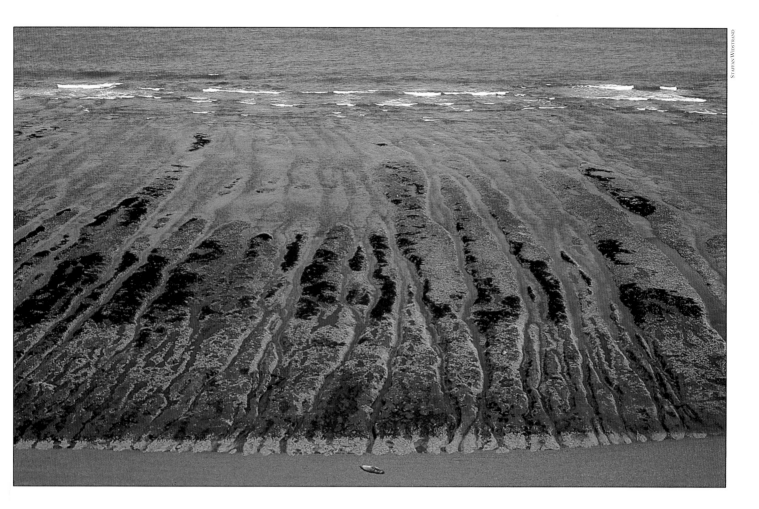

STAFFAN WIDSTRAND

Elephant Seals, Whales and Penguins
Peninsula Valdés and Punta Tombo, Patagonia, Argentina

The elephant seal's breath stinks of rotting fish and decaying seaweed. I venture too close and am blasted back on my heels by it. She awakes with a dreadful bellow, un-amused by my intrusion on her nap. I retreat, alarmed more by the stench than the noise coming from her vivid-pink mouth.

She shuts her eyes and appears as lifeless as before. The other seals lift sleepy eyelids, then close them. One seal in each group keeps watch, while the rest seem cast in concrete. I don't know why they need a watch-seal. On land they have no enemy apart from man, and they had let me come as close as 6.5 feet (2 m).

At this time of year, these ponderous animals are active only in the early morning and late evening, when they splash up and down in the water, thick layers of blubber quivering under their skins. The rest of the time they lie still. Perhaps now and again they scatter a little shingle over their bodies with their front flippers, but that's all. Things will liven up in a few weeks, when the adult males arrive to fight their bloody territorial battles and defend their harems.

Elephant seals and sea lions keep true harems. And they have to be defended with every ounce of their floppy weight and all the strength of their ungainly bodies.

The blubber which weighs them down in battle against their competitors has been their downfall in the struggle against their human persecutors.

Along the shores of the Valdés peninsula, you can still see the rusty remains of old factories which rendered seal blubber into oil, and the ruins of sealers' cabins. They date from the early nineteenth century, when men wiped out nearly all the elephant seals. They were easy to kill because they lived in big sedentary groups. Now they are a protected species, and their

99

STEFAN WIDSTRAND

numbers are slowly returning to their former level.

The Punta Tombo promontory features a huge colony of Magellanic penguins—little fellows in evening dress, 1.6 feet (0.5 m) tall and a good half a million in number—always on the move, in queues, in a hurry, in traffic jams, squabbling and hitting below the belt. The beaches where they swim, and clean themselves immediately afterward, resemble the seafront of a popular holiday resort. Although they look clumsy and silly on land, they are speedy in the water. They cannot fly, but in winter they migrate 600 miles (1000 km) north to the Brazilian coast, swimming all the way. Magellanic penguins are remarkably unafraid, and many pairs have their nests right beside the signposted path around the promontory. A long black-and-white procession of them waddles, wings outstretched, across the visitors' carpark, under a tourist bus, then down to the beach through a group of Japanese tourists.

Together with the elephant seals, they have become one the country's most popular tourist attractions, not least for the Argentinians themselves.

After spending several days watching her young, the female penguin is replaced at the nest by her mate and goes to sea to catch fish. First she cleans herself thoroughly (above), removing the dirt and dust of the nest from her feathers.

Told off by an irritated female elephant seal (opposite page) on the Valdés peninsula.

The Magellanic penguin colony at Punta Tombo (below) looks like a Swiss cheese.

The half-million penguins are constantly on the move. Long lines of them make their way like commuters going to work.

Penguins are not normally associated with a semi-desert climate of sun and heat—but much in nature is not as we imagine it to be. The most northerly penguins live on the Galápagos Islands, right on the Equator.

Description

Peninsula Valdés lies 93 miles (150 km) northeast of the town Trelew (which is about 373 miles [600 km] south of Buenos Aires). Valdés is a large peninsula, reaching out into the South Atlantic, where the cold waters of the Falkland Current, very rich in fish, surface along the coast of Patagonia. The countryside is almost uninhabited, very flat, arid, sparingly covered with bushes and big tufts of pampas grass. Animal life on land is very limited—with the exception of the odd group of guanacos, Patagonian maras and lesser rheas—but is so much more abundant on the shores and in the ocean. The gulf of *Golfo Nuevo* is, during the austral summer, a very important calving area for the rare southern right whale—one of the great baleen whales—and along the coastline of the peninsula there are several great rookeries of South American sea lions and southern elephant seals, numbering thousands of animals. Pods of killer whales come here regularly to hunt the young sea lions, and the Valdés Peninsula is one of the best places in the world to see these whales. Here is also found the place with the lowest elevation in South America, *Salinas Grandes*, a salt lake 138 feet (42 m) below sea level.

Reserva Faunística Punta Norte. The northern tip of the peninsula has a sea-lion rookery and many elephant seals. Some fences to keep the many visitors from disturbing the wildlife prevent close viewing. Best place for observing killer whales. These often take sea-lion pups, even from the beach, especially at high tide and in calm weather.

Reserva Faunística Isla de los Pajaros. Small islet in the Golfo San José, north of the peninsula, with masses of breeding seabirds. Cormorants, gulls, terns, ducks and shore-birds. The birdlife can be watched from the mainland at a good observation point.

Reserva Faunística Punta Pirámides. Sea-lion rookery on the steep coastline. The sea lions are observed almost from above.

Caleta Valdés, a 19-mile (30-km)-long ocean lagoon with an archipelago of gravel bars (see page 99), on the east coast of the peninsula. It is possible here to get closer to the elephant seals, while they are resting on the beach in their thousands. Also many Magellanic penguins.

Punta Cero (the south end of Caleta Valdés). Very good for elephant seals and penguins.

Reserva de Pingüinos de Punta Tombo. Comprising 52 acres (21 ha), 66 miles (107 km) southeast of Trelew. One of the largest colonies of Magellanic penguins, with at least 500,000 birds. A nature trail leads around to the best observation points. There is also a visitors' center. The rest of the reserve is closed. Those wishing to commune in solitude with the penguins would have to come early mornings or late afternoons, as the site is heavily visited.

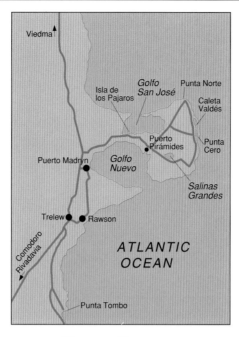

Fauna of interest

MAMMALS: Southern right whale (calving area in the Golfo Nuevo), killer whale (Punta Norte best), guanaco, Patagonian mara, southern elephant seal, South American sea lion, South American fur seal, Patagonian skunk, Argentine grey fox.

BIRDS: Magellanic penguin, giant petrel, lesser rhea, burrowing owl, snowy sheathbill, black-browed albatross, elegant-crested tinamou, flying steamer-duck, chubut steamer-duck, kelp gull, dolphin gull, royal tern, cayenne tern, peregrine falcon, great skua, king cormorant, rock shag, Guanay cormorant, turkey vulture, crested duck, great grebe.

Seasons

Southern right whale from July to November, best August to October. Killer whale from end of December to April, best February to April. Penguins breed September to March. Sea-lions pups are born in December/January. The weather during the austral summer is dry (rainfall only 8 inches/200 mm/year), windy and cool. During the austral winter, most of the wildlife is elsewhere.

How to get there

International flight to Buenos Aires. Domestic flight or bus to Trelew. Rented car from Trelew. From Puerto Pirámides to Punta Norte the distance is 47 miles (75 km).

Day excursions are organized daily. Transport is by bus from Trelew, but it usually arrives around midday to the coast, by which time all animal activity is very low.

Day excursions from Trelew to the penguins of Punta Tombo are better organized.

Daily whale-watching cruises depart for Golfo Nuevo from Puerto Pirámides in season. Often the whales can be seen at close hand. Diving among the whales is permitted.

Accommodation/food/camping

Hotels and restaurants in Trelew, Puerto Madryn and Puerto Pirámides, an excellent base for a few days on the Valdés Peninsula.

Other areas

The Iberá Swamps, Mesopotamia, Argentina. Vast areas of marshland, 93x31 miles (150x50 km), between the rivers Paraná and Paraguay. Wide plains, ranches, odd groves of trees, lakes, rivulets and canals. Herons, Maguari storks, ibises, roseate spoonbills, Jabiru storks, wattled jacanas, Muscovy ducks, American darters, 3 species of kingfishers, limpkins, capybaras, broad-snouted caimans, anacondas, brown brocket deer, armadillos, Pampas guinea-pigs. Tourism has just begun here. Travel from Concepción, Posadas or Corrientes.

Campos del Tuyú, Pampas, Argentina. WWF reserve with original, unspoiled wet pampas. Pampas deer, Argentine grey fox, capybara, Pampas guinea-pig, greater rhea, black-necked swan, Coscoroba swan, southern screamer, ovenbirds, chilean flamingo, Aplomado falcon, monk parakeet, crested caracara, roseate spoonbill, ibises, herons, grebes, 3 species of coots, burrowing owl, Everglade kite, long-winged harrier, American skimmer. For visits, contact the warden in nearby Gral Lavalle. There is also a large private ranch, *Estancia el Palenque*, just beside the WWF reserve. It has similar wildlife in similar habitat.

The lazy Valdés elephant seals tempt even the keenest eco-tourist to take a nap.

Kingdom of the Jaguar
The Manaus area, Amazonas, Brazil

At 5:00 A.M. the wail of howler monkeys wakes us in our hammocks on our little houseboat. It is pitch black outside, but high time to get up, for this is the most important hour of the day, when the animals and birds of the rainforest are most active.

The howler monkeys greet the dawn with a wave of sound like an oncoming train. Cicadas and crickets whir like little electric appliances, and hundreds of leaf frogs tinkle like delicate silver bells. At intervals we hear the swishing whistling of an insignificant gray bird, the screaming piha. This is most typical sound of the South American rainforest.

Brushing our teeth in the black water of the lagoon, we become aware of a large catfish, a good yard long, swimming on the surface by the boat. We'd like to catch it, but discover that it has already been caught.

During the night it has swallowed the cook's fish hook, with its bait of the previous day's chicken, and cannot get free. It will become fish fillets for lunch.

In the early-morning sunshine, patrol after patrol of magnificent blue-and-yellow macaws fly over us with frightful squawks. A pair of toucans sit whistling monotonously to each other in a dead tree. As they whistle they jerk their tails and their improbably large beaks like clockwork toys.

Silently our dugout canoe cleaves the smooth mirror of the water. A canopy of sparse treetops stretches above us; then, as we paddle on into the forest, mighty trunks rise around us. The eyes and nostrils of spectacled caimans project from a shady area. The previous night we shone powerful torches on the water and saw hundreds of their red eyes reflect back. When they are dazzled by the light, you can

STAFFAN WIDSTRAND

away. We do not find out, but in the evening, we hear his mighty territorial roars ring out from that area. So he had been near us.

They are cats who walk alone. Close to human habitation they sometimes stalk and kill horses, cattle, dogs and, occasionally, even humans. They come in many colors, from jet black to pure white, but are mostly an orange tan hue, spotted like their cousin, the leopard.

The spots, however, are slightly different from the leopard's. On the tail, they are arranged in rosettes with one spot in the center. Jaguars are about 4 feet (1.2 m) long from the nose to the root of the tail. They are less graceful in appearance than the leopard, more heavily built and with shorter legs, but just as agile and capable of great speed.

The deep, hoarse roar we heard is a night cry, rarely heard during the day, and used mostly in the mating season. Jaguar cubs mature rapidly, and can follow their mothers on the hunt when they are five weeks old.

About 6 percent of the rainforest in the state of Amazonas has been cut down. The rest is still there, sheltering its jaguars.

catch small ones by hand. Small wonder that they so quickly disappear around all human habitation.

Rainforest growing on firm ground is not as impassable on foot as many believe, but it is easy to get lost—it all looks much the same. The canopy of treetops, 115 feet (35 m) up, takes away most of the light, so vegetation down on the ground is sparse. Most of the birds and mammals, and even the plants, prefer to be up in the treetops.

Suddenly we spot jaguar tracks! First-rate footprints of the continent's largest predator. Tracks so fresh that water is still oozing into them. Perhaps the great cat was watching us from the bushes, a few yards

The spectacled caiman (opposite page) used to be found throughout the Amazonas wetlands. Unfortunately, it is easy to hunt and it has disappeared from inhabited areas. It is still to be seen in the shadier parts of the Rio Negro. It seldom grows to more than 10 feet (3 m) in length.

You seldom see the jaguar (above); usually you have to be content with seeing its tracks (right). But you might see one in the national parks of Manu in Peru, Jaú in Brazil, and the Mazaruni River in Guyana.

Water rising in the rainforest. Near Manaus, water levels vary by more than 50 feet (15 m) during the year. The profusion of forest-dwelling species here is amazing, but finding them takes patience. The vine snake (below) catches frogs and small birds in the trees and in bushes. The blue-crowned motmot (right) is distantly related to bee-eaters and kingfishers.

Description

The Amazon basin is bigger than the whole Indian subcontinent, and the Amazon River itself is the most powerful river on earth, counting for some 20 percent of all the fresh water reaching the world's oceans. Formally it starts here, at the junction of the mighty Rio Negro and Rio Solimões, just where Manaus city lies today.

Lowland rainforests in the Amazon basin are mainly of three different kinds. Firm ground forests, "Terra firme," covering about 90 percent of the surface, and the two types of periodically flooded forests, together covering some 2 percent, mainly along the largest rivers. Tremendous amounts of water are transported by these, from the rains on the eastern slopes of the Andes and the highlands of Venezuela and the Guyanas. In the city of Manaus the water level varies annually by over 50 feet (15 m)!

The trees of the flooded forests have adapted to a life where their roots and often great parts of their trunks stand under water for eight months or more a year. They are divided into Igapó and Várzea forests. *Igapó forests* grow in areas with dark, acid waters (looking a bit like strong tea), with low nutrient levels. *Várzea forests* grow where the water is neutral, rich in silt and nutrients, and looks like coffee with milk. The main rivercourses are quite straight, while many of the tributaries meander, creating oxbow lakes .

The area around Manaus is one of the most interesting in the Amazon and also one of the easiest to reach. The Várzea forests of the Rio Solimões and the Igapó forests of the Rio Negro are here where the two huge rivers join. The two very differently colored waters run side by side for several miles without mixing.

In the 19-mile (30-km) wide channel of the Rio Negro lies the **Anavilhanas Arquipelago**, probably the greatest fresh-water archipelago in the world. Along 56 miles (90 km) of the river are over 400 islands, most of them only 164 to 328 feet (50 to 100 m) across, but often several miles long. Their features change from year to year, and between the islands is a network of narrow natural canals. 1,352 square miles (3500 sq km) of the area have been set aside as an ecological reserve, *Estaçao Ecológica Anavilhanas*.

Monkeys and sloths are especially common here. *Ariaú* is an area rich in wildlife on the frequently flooded strip of land between the two big rivers. The pink Tucuxi dolphin is common here. The island *Ilha Papagaio* can only be seen during the low-water period from October to December, and is then a night roost for many hundreds of parrots of different species. Other good areas are *Ilha Tucuman, Lago Ubim, Rio Cuieiras* and *Rio Apuau.*

Farther away lies **Jaú National Park**, with the impressive size of 87,652 square miles (227 000 sq km) (!) of almost virgin Amazon rainforest. Wildlife there is extraordinary, and the species are roughly the same as in the Pantanal and in the Manu. There are as yet no

hotels or camps, or any infrastructure at all.

Around Manaus there is genuine rainforest, rich in wildlife, in every direction, just a few hours away from the city.

Fauna of interest

MAMMALS: Amazon manatee, Tucuxi dolphin, Amazon River dolphin, jaguar, ocelot, jaguarundi, Margay cat, puma, Brazilian tapir, giant anteater, southern tamandua, coati, capybara, red howler, black spider monkey, squirrel monkey, woolly monkey and several other monkeys, sloths, tayra, 4 species of armadillo.

BIRDS: More than 450 bird species, e.g., 12 species of heron (including boat-billed heron), green ibis, muscovy duck, 16 species of parrot (including blue-and-yellow macaw), sun bittern, hoatzin, horned screamer, hummingbirds, storks, toucans, guanos, curassows, king vulture, harpy eagle.

REPTILES: Spectacled caiman, black caiman, caiman lizard, iguana, anaconda, several species of boa.

FISH: Arapaima/pirarúcu (largest fresh-water fish in the world).

Seasons

All year round. Going on a boat trip during the high-water season (March to August) enables one to see many mammals at eye level, even when they sit in the treetops! The rainy season ends in February/March. Main tourist season is March to August. Driest season May to October. Low water in October/November. Manaus gets about 68 inches (1770 mm) of annual rainfall distributed over the year, but a little more during the rainy season. Greatest numbers of wintering birds here in January, especially in the Várzea forest.

How to get there

International flight to Rio de Janeiro, São Paulo or Brasília and then domestic flight to Manaus. Or direct flight from several South American capitals. From Manaus with boat or jeep.

Accommodation/food/camping

Manaus is center for a well-run eco-tourism business. All kinds of boat trips and lodging can be organized from here. Many houseboats are available, with captains and guides. Well-known lodges are: *Ariaú Jungle Tower* (130-foot (40-m)-high treetop hotel in the middle of the forest) and the *Apurrisawa Jungle Lodge*. The floating *Janauacá Jungle Lodge* lies in a lagoon southwest of Manaus, and the floating *Amazon Lodge* lies in the Lago Juma, straight south of Manaus. *Amazon Camp* lies in the rainforest east of Manaus. Excellent low-price alternatives are houseboat accommodation or sleeping in hammocks in wooden bungalows with straw roofs, so-called "*tapiris*".

Similar or nearby areas

Pantanal, Mato Grosso, Brazil. Comprising 88,810 square miles (230 000 sq km) of grass savannas, wetlands, lakes, rivers, forests and grazing lands. A prime ranching area with 6 million head of cattle. Jaguar, ocelot, puma, capybara, pampas deer, marsh deer, giant anteater, several species of armadillo, southern tamandua, coati, giant otter, maned wolf. 600 bird species, among them Jabiru stork, roseate spoonbill, greater rhea, red-legged seriema, southern screamer, king vulture, hyacinth macaw, blue-and-yellow macaw, red-and-green macaw, Toco toucan. Spectacled caiman, anaconda, caiman lizard. Most visitors in the dry season (May to November, best in September/October). Well-organized eco-tourism from Cuiabá, Corumbá and Campo Grande. The Cara Cara Ecological Reserve, south of Porto Joffre, is one of the most un-spoiled parts, very rich in wildlife. Lodges and *Fazendas* (ranches) provide lodging in the Pantanal. The *Pousada Caiman* lodge has a private reserve of 205 square miles (530 sq km). From the Trans-Pantaneira road between Poconé and Porto Joffre, many typical species can be sighted.

Hato Piñero, **Hato El Cedral** and **Hato El Frio**, Llanos, Venezuela. Wide grass savannahs, wetlands, gallery forests and hills with dry forests along the Orinoco River and its tributaries. Private cattle- and game-ranches/ research stations, which at the same time are hotels. Jaguar, ocelot, jaguarundi, puma, giant otter, Tucuxi dolphin, giant anteater, southern tamandua, crab-eating raccoon, red howler, Brazilian tapir, peccaries, white-tailed deer, capybara, tayra, armadillos, Amazon manatee. More than 325 species of birds, among them Jabiru stork, hoatzin, seven species of ibis (including scarlet ibis), roseate spoonbill, 17 species of heron, Orinoco goose. Common boa, anaconda, spectacled caiman, Orinoco crocodile, iguana. Dry season November to April best for visits. Most birds breed during the flooding season (May to September).

Nature's Laboratory
The Galápagos Islands, Ecuador

Suddenly it stands there in the raw, cold mist—500 pounds (227 kg) of Galápagos tortoise, a relic of primeval times, outrageously bowlegged and with a shell like a steel helmet, glistening with dew in the moonlight. Seeing it from below, from a wet sleeping-bag, comes as a shock. Evidently we have been sleeping in the hollow where it has spent every night for the last hundred years.

We are on the side of the crater of the 3,600-foot (1100-m) Alcedo volcano on the island of Isabela. The great reptiles lumber in the mists from one grazing place to the next. In the evenings they gather to sleep in the hollows, seeking from each other warmth and protection against the damp winds.

Sea mists roll in during the night, bringing moisture which condenses as dew on bushes and grass. As it is November, the dry season on the islands, all the Isabela tortoises have gathered to feed on the green vegetation. We see over a thousand in one day. "Galápagos" is Spanish for "tortoise," so they have given their name to the archipelago.

The prehistoric reptiles live on in much the way they have done for millions of years, lumbering about their business for part of the day and dozing through the rest of it.

It's a slow life, but a long one—possibly 150 years. What's encouraging about the Galápagos is that the sleepy giants are now being left to drowse in peace. In the early whaling days up to 10 million of them were killed as food for sailors.

We move on to the island of Española, where huge, bloated male sea lions give us a warm welcome even before our little motorboat reaches the shore.

STAFFAN WIDSTRAND

Bellowing, belching and snorting with jealous rage, they come wallowing toward us.

The grotesque males are as ugly as their females are supple and beautiful. Their anger is mostly for show—they are staking out limits—and we land safely a few yards from the nearest females. Minutes later, we are swimming with our masks and flippers, playing tag with them.

Blue-footed boobies breed farther up the island. One stands in the middle of the path, legs wide apart, dagger-shaped bill upward. It rivets us with its eyes and refuses to budge. I worry that the sharp bill will take a stab at the camera, but it sticks its head under its wing and goes to sleep on the spot.

We are forced to leave the path and go around the dauntless booby. Its companions are playing comical mating games on the lava rocks. They stand and stamp to show their bright blue feet, rub bills and bow to one another, ever deeper until they nearly twist themselves inside out.

The Galápagos archipelago is a remarkable collection of dry, stony, thorny and quite desolate semi-desert islands, glorious in their cactus flowers, yet stinking of dead fish and bird droppings. Everywhere there is life and death, but no palm trees, no tropical romance.

The islands confuse the senses by mixing beauty with nausea and color with stenches. But, despite the many visitors, there is no human litter and no commercialism.

Galápagos tortoises (above) and blue-footed boobies (right) are among the fearless inhabitants of these islands.

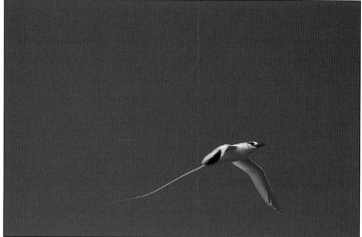

The red-billed tropicbird (above) is common to tropical seas, but the marine iguana (left) and the Galápagos tortoise (below) are found only on the Galápagos Islands. The marine iguana is a yard-long lizard and, despite its forbidding appearance, a peaceful vegetarian living on algae. The Galápagos tortoises, which can weigh over 440 pounds (200 kg), have been here for more than 5 million years.

Description

The Galápagos Islands, also called "the Enchanted Islands," consist of 13 larger and some 40 smaller islands; spread out over roughly 19,300 square miles (50 000 sq km) of the Pacific and situated almost right on the Equator, 620 miles (1000 km) from the South American mainland. The archipelago is about 186 miles (300 km) in diameter.

There are no terrestrial predators and very few birds of prey. The first men arrived in the 16th century; in greater numbers not until the 20th century. Consequently, wildlife has not had to develop protective behavior, and the animals are incredibly tame and not shy. Many species (about 50 percent of the breeding birds, 20 percent of the fishes and 40 percent of the plants) are endemic, and exist only here. Several species are restricted even to one single island. Hence the other name of these islands: "The Experiment Workshop of Nature." It is believed that the tortoises have lived here for at least 5–6 million years.

Galápagos has been a national park since 1959, and today about 18,000 people live there, most of them working with fishing and/or tourism, living in a few small communities. The number of visitors is said to be limited to 60,000 per year. All have to stick strictly to the organized trails, guided by competent local naturalists.

Tourism is carefully managed and is one of Ecuador's main sources of foreign currency. It is also the main reason why the islands have remained as preserved as they are. Here many countries, even in the industrialized world, have a great deal to learn about managing eco-tourism.

The fauna of the islands is the main attraction, but the underwater world here is also fascinating. It is possible to scuba-dive at the coral reefs, with sea lions and penguins swimming around at close distance.

Española (albatrosses), Santa Cruz (Charles Darwin Research station and Tortuga Negra Bay), Plazas, Isabela Punta Espinosa and Tagus Cove (with cormorants and penguins), Genovesa (red-footed boobies), North Seymour (frigatebirds), Santiago (black and red lava-sand beaches, a flamingo pool and Sullivan Bay), Floreana (Post Office Bay and the coral reefs of Corona del Diablo), Rábida (flamingos and swimming with sea lions), Bartholomeo (penguins).

Fauna of interest

MAMMALS: California sea lion, Galápagos fur seal, bottle-nosed dolphin, sperm whale (especially north of Fernandina).

BIRDS: Galápagos penguin, waved albatross, flightless cormorant, Hawaiian petrel, Audubon's shearwater, several species of storm petrel, masked booby, blue-footed booby, red-footed booby, red-billed tropicbird, great frigatebird, magnificent frigatebird, brown pelican, Chilean flamingo,

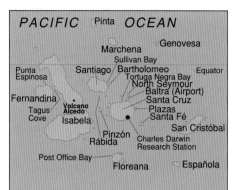

Galápagos hawk, lava heron, several endemic species of mockingbird and Galápagos finch, Galápagos dove, short-eared owl, swallow-tailed gull, lava gull, common noddy, Galápagos martin.

REPTILES AND AMPHIBIANS: Marine iguana, land iguana, Galápagos tortoise, green turtle, leatherback turtle, lava lizards.

FISH: Manta, hammerhead shark, whitetip shark, blacktip shark, stingray and hundreds of colorful tropical-fish species.

Seasons

Sea lions give birth in October/November. Birds breed all year round, but not all species all the time. The waved albatross breeds from April to November on Española. The hottest season is January to April, with high temperatures, warm water and generally clear skies. The rest of the year is the cooler season, the "garua," which brings cooler water 66°F (19°C), parts of the days overcast, air temperatures of 68–77°F (20–25°C) and sometimes a fine drizzle. Rainfall is always light and unreliable, heaviest at the coast April/May.

How to get there

International flight to Quito. Domestic flight via, or cruising ship from, Guayaquil. The ship is cheaper but takes almost two full days in each direction. Flights are often fully booked far in advance during high season. While there, one has to travel between the islands on boat, which is done either in a fleet of smaller "yachts" with space for 8–34 persons, or in luxury boats, carrying up to 90. The best nature experience is often achieved by going in one of the smaller vessels; their schedules are a little more flexible and one does not have to line up and wait for

everything, as is often the case with the larger ships. Since the number of visitors is limited, it is a good idea to book well in advance. At the latest from Quito or Guayaquil before the departure for Galápagos, but preferably even earlier.

Accommodation/food/camping

Galápagos is expensive. The only way to get around the islands is to join an organized cruise, or to hire a whole boat oneself. On the cruises everything is included—food, transport, lodging on board, the compulsory naturalist guide, cook and boat crew. Local operators vary from decent to excellent; prices also vary, not always accordingly. Which of them offers the best value for the money is difficult to know beforehand. Most eco-tourist travel agents sell good deals. About a full week is required so that you don't feel you have to chase around or exclude important islands. Camping is allowed only with a special permit, and this at a very limited number of sites.

Other areas

Reserva Faunística de Cuyabeno. The best lowland rainforest area in Ecuador, with almost virgin Amazon rainforest around the junction of the Río Napo and Río Aguarico. Here you can find monkeys of more than 10 species, jaguars, Brazilian tapirs, sloths, kinkajous, coatis, two species of caimans, at least 600 species of birds (among them king vulture, harpy eagle, hoatzin and macaws), arapaima (largest freshwater fish in the world), Amazon river dolphins, Amazon manatee. Lodging in *Sacha Lodge, Cuyabeno Lodge, Cuyabeno River Shelter, Iripari Lodge* or *Imuya Camp.* Zancudococha and Lagartococha are probably the two most rewarding lakes to visit. Visits can be booked from Quito.

Parque Nacional de Cotopaxi. Its 319 square miles (825 sq km) contain one of the world´s most perfectly conical volcanoes, 19,118 feet (5827 m) high, with interesting high-altitude fauna and flora. On the high plateau in front of the volcano there is a lake, teeming in birds. Raptors, hummingbirds, ducks, Andean lapwings, Andean gulls, white-tailed deer, Culpeo foxes and more. Sometimes the Andean condor is sighted. Easily reached by rented car from Quito.

Cerro Antisana/Santuario del Cóndor. Antisana is another snow-covered volcano, 18,714 feet (5704 m) high, with species similar to those of Cotopaxi, but nature here is more undisturbed. In addition, this is the best place in Ecuador to see the Andean condor. Antisana lies closer to Quito than does Cotopaxi. Best highland bird area in the country. Private reserve of 714 square miles (1850 sq km).

It may look dangerous, but the Galápagos tortoise is vegetarian and interested only in the photographer's sandwich.

HASSE SCHRÖDER

Alligators and Herons
Everglades National Park, Florida, USA

Approaching Miami international airport, our plane makes a wide sweep over the southern tip of Florida. The country below is utterly flat. The vast swampland of the Everglades stretches seemingly forever. Its water glistens in the sunlight; its dark groves contrast with pale yellow sedge. No houses to be seen; Florida looks like an uninhabited wilderness.

Minutes later, we land in Miami, to find a great, chaotic mix of people—the Caribbean, Central America and the USA all delightfully conglomerated amid multilane highways, skyscrapers and large harbors for private craft. The exhaust-shrouded city of 12 million inhabitants is as far from primordial nature as can be imagined. Yet it takes less than an hour by car to find calm in the endless marshlands.

In Shark Valley a 13-foot (4-m) alligator waits in the shallows. Wet patches on the path, the shape of an alligator, and the outline of a tail in the sand, demonstrate that she has just been lying on land. Now only her eyes and blunt snout show above the clear water, where she appears to be standing on the bottom. Now her knobbed back comes to the surface. She is obviously annoyed by my curiosity, and her facial expression changes. A menacing, toneless growl emerges through the bared teeth, then is repeated as froth forms around her jaws. I retreat a few steps.

A flock of frightened wood storks and white ibises flies up and disappears into the distance. With all my senses concentrated on the alligator's next reaction, I am caught off guard by an authoritative voice behind me.

"Don't go any closer!"

A uniformed woman park warden, with a Magnum revolver in her belt and a broad-brimmed hat on her head, is surprised by my reaction.

"Pardon me. I didn't mean to startle you. But this

alligator gets annoyed very easily now as she has young ones. The young won't be far away."

When I step back farther, the great reptile calms down, but keeps watchful eyes just above the surface. Little alligators, scarcely more than a foot (30 cm) long, appear. There must be a dozen, but I can't count them, for they swim about and dive the whole time. The mother shows no warm maternal feelings, but there is no doubt that she looks after them.

To some people alligators may not be the most appealing of creatures. They demand respect because they are certainly among the oldest of creatures— their ancestry can be traced back to Jurassic times. And they get respect because most of us prefer not to mess around with them.

Crocodilians, which include alligators and caymans, are the world's largest reptiles. The sea-going saltwater kind can grow to more than 20 feet (6 m) in length.

The big alligator I met only growled at me, but in the mating season the males bellow loud enough to be heard from a considerable distance. Their chief enemy is man, who has slaughtered much of the American alligator population for leather shoes and handbags, so they usually avoid full-grown humans. But they regularly snatch dogs from river banks, and small children playing in shallow water are potentially in danger. In March, 1997, a three-year-old boy was taken and drowned by an alligator in a Florida lake. Since 1948, when official state recording began, there have been 225 such attacks on humans in Florida. Only seven have been fatal.

Ahead of us, fifty vultures circle a clump of trees. When we get there, we find a huge dead alligator lying half underwater, with a dozen vultures tearing out its entrails.

The thickness of the coruscations along its back indicate that it is, or was, a large and very old animal, perhaps one of the few Everglades alligators that grow to more than 16 feet (5 m).

Another big jet flies over, on its way to Miami. We wonder how many of its passengers know that one of North America's most famous national parks is right below them.

In the subtropical Everglades (left), the alligator (above) comes up on dry land in daytime to warm itself in the sun. Although it may look dead, it keeps a watchful eye open.

MAGNUS ELANDER

Tidal shores, mangrove forests and freshwater swamps are the haunts of birds that include the egret (above) and the Louisiana heron (left). The puma (below) lives in all kinds of habitats, from deserts, rainforests and inaccessible mountain areas to the Everglades marshes. A few pumas, locally known as "Florida panthers," are still found in the northern parts of the national park, and in the adjoining Big Cypress National Preserve.

MAGNUS ELANDER

JOHN CANCALOSI

Description

Everglades National Park, on the southern tip of the Florida peninsula, was established in 1947 and covers 2,185 square miles (5660 sq km) of totally flat subtropical wetlands. Rock Reef Pass, 3 feet (0.9 m) above sea level, is one of the highest points. The park is mainly divided into three different habitats. A marine archipelago in the far south, a mangrove-covered delta along the coast and the interior with extensive sawgrass-covered freshwater swamps.

Florida Bay has an archipelago where the Mexican Gulf meets the Atlantic, with low mangrove-covered islets and coral reefs. This is the home of the rare manatee, or sea cow. The osprey is a typical sight in the air and on the water, and there are frequently large flocks of wintering American white pelicans. Some 50 pairs of bald eagles nest along the coast. Myriads of shorebirds winter on the tidal shores, while herons and roseate spoonbills are seen at all seasons.

A broad border zone between the sea and the mainland is covered by mangroves, a haunt for masses of white ibises, herons and wood storks. This is also the habitat of the threatened American crocodile. Wilderness Waterway, a popular 99-mile (160-km)-long canoe trail through the mangroves, connects the visitors' centers in Everglades City and Flamingo.

The interior is mainly a flat sea of sawgrass with islands of strangler fig, royal palm, gumbo limbo trees and, in a few places, more continuous low bald cypress stands. A classical impassable swamp with tall bald cypress with submerged roots and covered by epiphytic orchids and other plants on the trunks is best seen in Big Cypress National Preserve, next-door neighbor to the north.

The Everglades is percolated by a fresh-water river, only 6 inches (15 cm) deep but 50 miles (80 km) wide. It trickles rather than flows toward the sea in Florida Bay on a riverbed that slopes ever so gradually. Along its long course from its sources in central Florida, the water drops only 15 feet (4.6 m). Lack of water is a threat to the Everglades. The rapidly growing population in south Florida consumes an increasing share of the fresh-water—siphoned off from its natural course through the national park into wide manmade canals. The consequences are immediately measurable in the dramatic decrease of wetland birds. Although birdlife still seems prosperous, it is estimated that only one-tenth of the original numbers of certain species remains.

Fauna of interest

BIRDS: Roseate spoonbill, wood stork, white ibis, glossy ibis, limpkin, 2 species of pelicans, anhinga, 12 species of herons, bald eagle, snail kite, American swallow-tailed kite, black vulture, turkey vulture, fulvous whistling-duck.

MAMMALS: Manatee (or sea cow), puma,

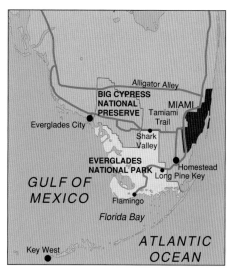

whitetail deer, river otter, common opossum, raccoon, nine-banded armadillo.

REPTILES: American alligator, American crocodile.

Seasons

All year, but best from November through March. The rainy season, from mid-April to mid-December, brings warm weather combined with high humidity. Clouds of mosquitoes are prone to make visits a nightmare. June to November means a risk of running into severe hurricanes. Dry season is definitely the most pleasant and, due to the low water level, birds flock around the remaining waterholes and are easier to spot.

How to get there

International or domestic flight to Miami or Ft. Lauderdale. By car 55 miles (89 km), via Homestead to the southern entrance to the national park, open 24 hours. From the visitors' center there are 38 miles (61 km) of paved roads through the park to the visitors' center at Flamingo, the starting point for most activities in the park. The roads, and the hiking trails or canoe trails starting from various points along the road, are excellent for wildlife

Turkey vulture

viewing. Everything, from bikes and canoes to houseboats, may be rented at Flamingo, and guided tours by boat start from here. The northern entrance at Shark Valley is reached by car, 31 miles (50 km) from Miami via the Tamiami Trail. A 15-mile (24-km)-long road looping out into the sea of sawgrass offers excellent opportunities for close-up views of alligators and the large wetland birds. Driving is prohibited, but walking, riding a rental bike or joining guided tours by bus several times a day leaves ample choice. The third entrance is via Everglades City in the far northwest, and from here a boat is a must. Everything can be rented and there are daily guided tours by boat during the dry season into the mangroves and the archipelago. Wilderness Waterway is a canoe trail connecting Everglades City to Flamingo. Airboats scare away all wildlife and are prohibited within the park, but are very popular outside.

Accommodation/food/camping

Flamingo Lodge is the only hotel within the park. Hotels/motels are found in Homestead, Florida City, Miccousukee and Everglades City just outside the park. Two camping grounds in Flamingo and Long Pine Key for tents as well as camper-vans. Eating-places and store in Flamingo and Shark Valley. In Everglades City there is a wide selection of services. Overnight camping along canoe and hiking trails requires a permit, obtainable at any visitors' center.

Other areas

Okefenokee National Wildlife Refuge, Georgia, USA, comprising 540 square miles (1400 sq km). A pristine swamp area with giant bald cypress and dense undergrowth. All vegetation grows on a thick layer of peat with no contact with the underlying bedrock; thus the American natives named it "land of trembling earth." American alligator, black bear, raccoon, river otter, whitetail deer, sandhill crane, herons, ibises, fulvous whistling-duck, anhinga, wild turkey. The area is best negotiated by boat.

Crystal River National Wildlife Refuge, Florida, USA. Snorkeling with manatees (sea cows) under supervision of experienced guides.

Caroni Swamp, Trinidad. Mangroves and lagoons. Night-roost for thousands of scarlet ibises, masses of herons (e.g., boat-billed herons and yellow-crowned night-herons), owlet-nightjars, anhingas. Spectacled caimans. Tours by boat every afternoon.

Asa Wright Nature Centre, Trinidad. A former cacao plantation with excellent highland rainforest. Cave with nesting *Steatornis caipensis*. Trogons, white bellbirds, jacamars, raptors, owls, toucans, 12 species of hummingbirds, parrots. Professional birding guides. Tours to all nature areas on the island available.

Bison and Wapiti
Yellowstone National Park, Wyoming, USA

The October air is cold and crystal-clear. At 6,500 feet (2000 m) above sea level, the Madison River skirts the Rocky Mountain watershed. The early snow has thawed, but the temperature drops again as the sun sinks behind the straggling branches of lodgepole pines and Engelmann spruces. Trumpeter swans call faintly, and Canada geese flap along the river. A gray jay sounds a warning note, and two fly-fishing tourists run toward us, still in their wet waders. "Bison!" they shout. "Masses of them, wading across the river!"

Through binoculars, we can make out several the dry, yellow grass on the riverbanks, others standing, drinking in the water. A couple of young bulls measure each other's strength like Sumo wrestlers. They stand with heads down, forehead to forehead, their horns interlocked. When the stronger one has forced his opponent back over an invisible line, or, better still, into the water, the contest is over. Other bulls are running amok, unleashing their fighting urge on the trees. Their horns rip long strips of bark off the pines and push young trees over.

The bison was the symbol of the North American prairies. They may in fact have created the prairies. Sixty million of them roamed the Midwest cropping all young shoots, trampling down any embryo forest and

Only a handful survived the massacre. Even in the wild, inaccessible Yellowstone country there were only thirty-nine bison left at the end of the nineteenth century. These are the founders of the present herd, now three thousand strong.

Forest fires are part of the natural cycle in Yellowstone. But in the late summer of 1988, the worst conflagration in its history destroyed nearly half the park, and it seemed that the animals and the vegetation would never recover. The effect was the opposite. The fires created a mosaic of new habitats, and Yellowstone experienced an explosion of biological renewal and rejuvenation. The bison and wapiti population fell by nearly 20 percent in the short term, but grizzlies and black bears were not affected at all. And the flow of tourists is growing steadily. Park signs warn them to stay away from the bison, which are wild and dangerous. But they simply have to see these impressive beasts who once ruled the territory. This is one of the biggest herds left in the world, but still a poor remnant of what once was.

They will never regain their importance to life in America, but they are beginning to regain their correct name. Despite the fame of the Wild West showman William "Buffalo Bill" Cody (1846–1917) he never met an actual buffalo. They all live in Africa or India.

He did kill thousands of American bison, a different zoological species, when he was a Pony Express

leaving an endless grass plain. Thus the bison shaped its own environment—perhaps with the help of the 40 or 50 million pronghorn antelopes that also lived here.

The American prairie Indians lived off the bison. Clothes and tents were made from the hides. The flesh provided both fresh meat and the raw material for jerky and pemmican, preserved forms of bison meat. When European settlers arrived, bison hides became a trading commodity. Every year hundreds of thousands were exchanged for ammunition, beads and whiskey. When the railroads brought many more white men, the slaughter was without parallel. Fortune seekers used rifles that could bring down an animal at more than a mile, and they had no chance of survival.

The immigrants believed they had an inexhaustible source of meat, hides and leather, but they soon exhausted it. The bison, more often called "buffalo," were killed for pleasure, and their carcasses left to rot.

October is the breeding season for bison, and the bulls roar continuously as they tear through forest and meadowland. Violent duels on the riverbank (below) decide their order of precedence. The bison, or buffalo, was once the most common large prairie animal in North America.

Traces of the great forest fire of 1988 still remain (above), but the devastation brought about a rejuvenation of vegetation, and was actually a benefit to wildlife.

zoological species, when he was a Pony Express rider and meat supplier to the builders of the Union Pacific Railroad. The meat was comparable to that of domestic beef cattle.

"Buffalo Bill's" victims were prairie bison, slightly smaller than the woodland kind but still massive animals, weighing up to 2000 pounds (909 kg). European bison once roamed the whole of that continent, but are now to be found only in zoos.

America has been more fortunate. At least a few of them remain in their wild state as a reminder of their former glory.

The wapiti (left) is a large North American species of deer and the most common ungulate in Yellowstone. It has recovered quickly and is at least as numerous as before the fire. Yellowstone is an excellent example of how tourist pressure can protect wildlife while offering a genuine experience of it.

118

Description

Yellowstone National Park, established in 1872, is the oldest national park in the world. The park is located in the Rocky Mountains at an elevation of 6,562 feet (2000 m) or more, and covers almost 3,475 square miles (9000 sq km) of spectacular wilderness with mountains (highest is Eagle Peak, at 11,358 feet/3462 m), lakes, rivers, canyons and waterfalls. Three-quarters of the park is covered by forest, mostly lodgepole pine. In addition there are large areas with geysers (c. 200) and hot springs. The magnificent scenery has the largest concentration of terrestrial wildlife in the USA (apart from Alaska). Hayden Valley is a rewarding place to watch bison and moose, as is Lamar Valley, where encounters with elks, pronghorns, and even coyotes are frequent. Bighorn sheep are often observed between Mammoth and Gardiner, Montana, and pronghorns in the vicinity of the northern entrance. The best place to see elk is between Mammoth and Madison. Although the bear population is not decreasing, grizzly and black bear are not observed as often as previously. There are no garbage-can bears any more. Rangers regularly transfer bears attracted to areas with human activities into more remote parts of the park. The park is one of the world's most frequented, with hundreds of thousands of visitors annually. In spite of this, as soon as cars and main roads are left behind, pristine wildlife and adventures are waiting around the corner.

Fauna of interest

MAMMALS: Grizzly bear, black bear, puma, bison, moose, elk, mule deer, bighorn sheep, pronghorn, coyote, North American porcupine, American beaver, river otter, American marten, mink, snowshoe hare, yellowbellied marmot, pika.

BIRDS: Bald eagle, osprey, red-tailed hawk, peregrine falcon, great gray owl, American white pelican, trumpeter swan, sandhill crane, Canada goose, harlequin duck, blue grouse, ruffed grouse, gray jay, Clark's nutcracker.

Seasons

All year, but best for the large mammals during spring and autumn, with fewer visitors. Autumn is also rutting time for bison and elk. Summer means daily highs of 68°F (20°C) and nightly lows at freezing point. From October 31 through May 1, most roads and entrances are closed by snow. The northern entrances are, however, kept open all year, and the road connecting them is good for spotting wildlife. Snowmobiles may be used on winter roads, and guided tours by snowcoach are available in the cold season. Most visitors in July and August.

How to get there

International flight to Seattle, Washington, or other international US airports with domestic service to Idaho Falls, Idaho; Billings,

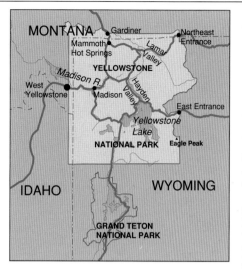

Montana; or Jackson, Wyoming. Continue by rental car or by bus. Yellowstone has nearly 310 miles (500 km) of public roads that, together with 994 miles (1600 km) of hiking trails, cover most parts of the park. There is plenty of wildlife along the roads. During autumn and spring, some roads may be closed due to snow. Off-road vehicles are not permitted.

Accommodation/food/camping

Within Yellowstone there are hotels, lodges and cabins at some ten locations. Less expensive accommodation is available outside the park, e.g., West Yellowstone, also an excellent base from which to make day trips into the park. Generally open from May/June to September/October. Restaurants and stores in connection with lodging. The store in Mammoth is open all year. Most camping grounds are kept open only in the summer, but a few are open all year. A permit is required for overnight camping and is available free of charge at any ranger station.

Trumpeter swan

Other areas

Waterton–Glacier National Park, Montana, USA, and Alberta, Canada. Comprising 1,700 square miles (4400 sq km) of breathtaking wilderness in the Rocky Mountains; includes forests, mountains with peaks above 9,842 feet (3000 m), 650 lakes, dozens of glaciers and countless waterfalls and cascades. The main attraction is some 600 grizzly bears, black bears, gray wolves, mountain goats, bighorn sheep, coyotes, moose, elk, mule deer, American beaver, wolverines. 200 different species of birds can be seen.

National Elk Refuge, Wyoming, USA, 37 square miles (97 sq km) at 6,562 feet (2000 m), less than 12 miles (20 km) north of Jackson, is wintering territory for 7,000–9,000 elk migrating here each autumn from Grand Teton National Park and surrounding areas. One of the last major seasonal migrations of large mammals in the USA. November is the best time to watch. The animals stay in the refuge November through April. In addition there are moose, bighorn sheep, mule deer and coyote. Visitors' center but no accommodation.

Grand Teton National Park, Wyoming, USA. Established in 1929. Located in the Rocky Mountains immediately south of Yellowstone, it has fewer visitors but similar wildlife. Pronghorn, elk, moose, beaver, trumpeter swan and sandhill crane. No bison, however.

Wood Buffalo National Park, Alberta, Canada, 17,183 square miles (44 500 sq km), on the border between Alberta and the Northwest Territories, is the largest national park in Canada. The landscape is typical of northern Canada, with large forests, extensive prairies, marshes, lakes and an almost total lack of humans. Renowned for housing North America's largest herd of free-roaming bison (4,200 animals). It is nowadays largely a hybrid herd from original wood bison and artificially added plains bison. Camping ground.

MAGNUS ELANDER

A Place of Eagles and Geese
Tule Lake, California, USA

It is 4:00 A.M. on a mid-November day—two and a half hours before sunrise. The thermometer shows 24°F (–4°C). The starry sky and waning moon provide barely enough light to behold the spectacle unfolding above us.

The air vibrates with the cackling of geese and the beating of their wings. Tens of thousands of them are arriving or departing all at once. Huge flocks on their way out from their night roosts on Tule Lake call to incoming geese that have spent the night grazing on the surrounding fields. Unceasingly, they fly over. The sky lightens to an unreal orange hue, revealing birds in every conceivable formation. The heavens are filled with lines astern and aslant, vee-formations, follow-my-leader alignments and other geometric patterns.

Colors and details of plumage appear. Pure white snow geese, with their coal-black wingtips, are in the majority, followed by hordes of white-fronted geese and cackling geese—a race of small Canada geese. A few weeks before my visit, wardens at the nature reserve reckoned there were 150,000 geese in the area. Now there are close to 200,000, plus a million ducks.

The Mount Shasta volcano sleeps in the background—15,000 feet (4317 m) high and permanently snow-capped. The flocks of snow geese on Tule Lake match its whiteness and spread like drift-ice. Most of them rest during the day in the middle of the lake. There are two kinds—the larger snow goose and the smaller Ross's goose. They breed in the far north of Canada and in Siberia, and stay around Tule Lake for a few weeks on their way to their winter quarters in the agreeable climate of central California. It is not easy to get close to such an enormous flock, but a bald eagle comes to my aid. When it appears, about 50,000 birds take to the wing.

A solitary bald eagle is enough to scare a hundred thousand snow geese into the air (opposite page), but when the danger has passed they all return to where they had been sleeping on Tule Lake. The geese feed on the surrounding cultivated land, some of which is set apart for their use. Some shooting is allowed there. In autumn there are more geese here than anywhere else in North America.

The 15,000-foot (4317-m) volcano Mount Shasta forms a backdrop to the Tule Lake nature reserve. The surrounding high plateau is rich in wildlife, including mule deer (overleaf above). It is a resting place for enormous flocks of snow geese on their way to and from their Arctic breeding grounds (overleaf below).

Why were 50,000 large birds so terrified of one solitary bird?

I'm sure any goose could tell you, and many humans, too. There is a stately magnificence about the approach of an eagle which has impressed soldiers and kings down the ages, and made this supreme bird of prey a symbol of power.

Likenesses of eagles are found on Greek and Roman ruins and many nations, including the United States, have adopted it as their national emblem.

When falconry was at its height in Europe, only kings were allowed to fly eagles. Eastern rulers used them to capture antelopes.

The stern, frowning bald eagle is a fierce-looking species. It is not bald, but gets its name from its peculiar flat-topped, white-plumed head. Frightening as it appears to other birds, its main diet is fish.

When it had gone they all came back together to alight on the lake. Geese fell like snow from the clouds, making a deafening noise with their cackling. How they find a free spot to land or avoid collisions in the confusion of wings and bodies, I fail to understand. But in a few minutes all are in their places again and calm has descended on Tule Lake.

Magnus Flander

Description

Tule Lake National Wildlife Refuge, on the border between California and Oregon in western USA, is one of six sanctuaries included in the Klamath Basin National Refuges. The refuge was established in 1928 and includes 58 square miles (150 sq km) of mainly lakes and farmland. The lakes and the surrounding wetlands are renowned for the immense numbers of waterfowl during autumn migration and for the largest congregation of wintering bald eagles in the USA, outside Alaska.

Tule Lake is located along the Pacific Flyway, i.e., the airway connecting the arctic breeding grounds in northern Canada and eastern Siberia with the wintering areas farther south in North America. The birds follow the same routes year after year and use the same stop-over places. It is not unusual to see a quarter of a million snow geese in a single day, and 80 percent of the world's Ross's geese migrate through the Klamath Basin.

Less than a hundred years ago, nearly 6 million ducks and geese used to stop-over here. In spite of the fact that only one-quarter of the original wetlands remains today after devastating drainage and gradual lowering of the water level in this century, more waterfowl congregate here in the late autumn than anywhere else in North America.

The bald eagle does not actually nest in the Tule Lake refuge, but only in the surrounding areas, where some 50 pairs are resident.

Bear Lake National Wildlife Refuge, 25 miles (40 km) west of Tule Lake, is one of the five most important night roosts for the eagles. In a few sturdy trees up to 300 eagles gather in the evenings to sleep. Bear Lake is closed to visitors, but when the eagles leave their roosts just before dawn, they can be seen at Worden, Oregon, along Highway 97. They fly at low altitude in a spectacular string-of-beads right across the road toward the hunting grounds at the lakes on the plains.

Fauna of interest

BIRDS: Snow goose, Ross's goose, Canada goose (subspecies: cackling goose), white-fronted goose; tundra swan; ducks representing most North American species in hundreds of thousands, including hooded merganser; bald eagle, golden eagle, northern harrier, buzzards, prairie falcon; American white pelican.

MAMMALS: Mule deer, pronghorn, muskrat, coyote.

Seasons

Ducks all year round. Geese from September and throughout winter, most numerous in November. Bald eagles from November until March/April, peaking in January/February. Sometimes up to 1,100 at the same time. Between 1,000 and 2,000 northern harriers are counted each winter. Pronghorns migrate

through the area in the late autumn, whereas mule deer, muskrats and coyotes are seen all year.

How to get there

International flight to San Francisco or Seattle. Domestic air to Klamath Falls, Oregon. Rental cars available. From Klamath Falls south to Hatfield, west on Road 161 a few miles, and then road signs guide the way to the visitors' center. Besides up-to-date information on geese and eagles, access to permanent photo blinds can be booked here. The Tule Lake refuge is easily negotiated and roads crisscross the area. Gravel roads on the elevated dikes bordering the pools and lakes offer excellent opportunities for close-up encounters with mammals and birds.

Accommodation/food/camping

The refuge is open only in daylight. Camping is not permitted. No accommodation within the refuge. Ellis Motel south of Hatfield is the only alternative to hotels or motels in Klamath Falls, Oregon.

Other areas

Sacramento National Wildlife Refuge, California, one hour north of Sacramento on Interstate 5. The refuge in the Sacramento Valley is extremely flat and the scenery is not comparable to Tule Lake's, but it is considerably easier to get to and closer to San Francisco. Large congregations of migrating waterfowl in autumn and winter, but only occasional bald and golden eagles.

J. Clark Salyer National Wildlife Refuge, North Dakota, USA, 93 square miles (240 sq km), located about 37 miles (60 km) northeast of Minot. In the autumn up to 150,000 snow geese are seen, 10,000 Canada geese, 2,000 tundra swans and 150,000 ducks.

Platte River–Big Bend Reach, Nebraska, USA. A 62-mile (100-km)-long stretch of the river between Grand Island and Lexington is a stop-over area for 250,000 sandhill cranes during spring migration. Optimal time is the

second half of March. Best viewing spots are in the vicinity of Kearney.

Chilkat River, Alaska, USA, about 19 miles (30 km) north of Haines. The best area for bald eagles in North America. From October to December up to 3,000 eagles gather within a very limited area.

Horicon National Wildlife Refuge, Wisconsin, USA. Comprising 33 square miles (85 sq km) wetlands and farmland, less than 62 miles (100 km) northeast of Madison. Stop-over area for large numbers of waterfowl and some 200,000 Canada geese, the largest congregation in North America. Worthwhile visiting from mid-September to December, best during the first half of October.

Squaw Creek National Wildlife Refuge, Missouri, USA. Comprising 11 square miles (28 sq km) wetlands near Mound City, with 350,000 snow geese and 100,000 ducks from mid-October to mid-November. In the wintertime there are about 300 bald eagles.

Aransas National Wildlife Refuge, Texas, USA. Comprising 85 square miles (220 sq km) of mainly tidal shores and salt marshes. Higher elevated areas are dotted with small lakes and lakelets. More than 350 species of birds have been observed, e.g., ibises, herons, sandhill cranes, roseate spoonbills. Famous wintering area for the highly threatened whooping crane. American alligator, whitetail deer, collared peccary and coyote.

The bald eagle, national emblem of the United States. Every winter more than a thousand of them are attracted to the land around Tule Lake, which teems with ducks and geese. This is the biggest concentration of eagles in North America, except for Alaska.

Island of Giant Bears
Kodiak National Wildlife Refuge, Alaska, USA

Rancher Bill Burton owned Alaska's largest breeding bull. He hired it out for rodeos, but no one could ever ride the 2,645-pound (1200-kg) angry giant. One day the bull met his match. A male bear got in through the fence and broke the bull's neck with one blow. It was dead in seconds. The Kodiak bear seldom uses its strength against humans; there are only a few recorded attacks in which people have been killed. But it can play havoc with cattle. So Bill and some of the other ranchers have switched from beef cattle to bison. "Better to adapt to the bears than fight them," he says.

Although the bison have been raised in captivity, they still have their natural defensive reactions and can hold their own much better against the giant bears. The Kodiak bear can be twice the size of a grizzly, and as big as the largest polar bear. A male standing on its hind legs is up to 13 feet (4 m) tall and weighs 1,760 pounds (800 kg).

From our camp site in the O'Malley River valley, we observe two families of bears who are spending the summer there.

There are two females, each with three cubs, and every day they live well on salmon. They don't wander far, because the fish is plentiful and easy to catch. The she-bears and cubs are most active during the daylight hours; at night they all rest close together in some hollow or under the dense osier beds along the river's edge. These windless late-summer mornings the bear cubs wake first and get into the water. Inexperienced, they walk haphazardly among the salmon without managing to catch a single one. Then the mother bear comes out and demonstrates her skill.

First she puts her whole head under the water to locate the fish. Then she stands up on her hind legs and throws herself at full length after them. Fish that avoid a direct hit from her sharp claws are caught in her jaws. In two hours she has eighteen big ones.

STEFAN QVINTH

You can never feel relaxed near these great bears. One afternoon, the female starts to move along the riverbank toward us, and we withdraw, gently and quietly, to show our inferiority and avoid any trial of strength. She rears up and glowers for a moment, then goes back to catching fish. We don't try to run away, because the bears are astonishingly quick and expert at moving through the brushwood. Flight would stimulate their hunting instincts.

In summer and late autumn, four species of salmon migrate up the rivers and streams to spawn. The most beautiful is the crimson-colored sockeye. Millions of fish crush into the smaller watercourses until the shallow water boils with them. The bears gorge themselves, putting a couple of hundred pounds of fat on their bodies—enough to see them through their hibernatory fast.

The solitary males are wanderers, covering many miles a day. They are not wanted at home, where the females become violent if they think their cubs are threatened. Only at dusk do the males go fishing. Our last picture of the O'Malley River is of a huge male bear, with the water rushing around his legs and a wildly struggling, fiery-red sockeye salmon in his jaws.

The salmon was doomed.

It was approaching the end of its tremendous journey across the Pacific, back up its native river and then its native stream to give life to the next generation of salmon, and then to die there.

It didn't quite make it, but neither did so many other of the beautiful red fish. Its legacy was its contribution to the survival of a gigantic bear—the king of Kodiak—who still reigns here.

In summer the world's largest brown bear, the Kodiak, lives almost entirely on salmon. As millions of spawning fish migrate up the rivers and streams, the bears enjoy a feast (above). The sockeye (right) is one of four salmon species that spawn in the watercourses of Kodiak Island.

STEFAN QUINTH

HAKAN NUNSTEDT

Every bear has its own style of fishing, and practice brings skill. The older bears are better at catching fish than the young are. One full-grown female caught eighteen big salmon in less than two hours.

HAKAN NUNSTEDT

Description

The Kodiak archipelago, south of the Alaska Peninsula, is slightly farther north than Glasgow. The major island is Kodiak Island, separated from the mainland by the 25-mile (40-km)-wide Shelikof Strait. Kodiak National Wildlife Refuge, comprising more than 3,089 square miles (8000 sq km), was established in 1941 and covers two-thirds of Kodiak Island and parts of neighboring Afognak Island. The refuge is completely off the beaten track. Access is by seaplane or boat only. The multitude of inlets and narrow fjords that penetrate deeply into the interior leaves no part of the land farther away from the sea than 16 miles (25 km). Along the rocky coast there are about 200 pairs of bald eagles nesting, and on many rocky islets there are auk colonies and sea-lion rookeries. From the mountain peaks at 4,920 feet (1500 m) down to the shores, the island in summer is carpeted in various shades of green. The northern part is covered by Sitka spruce forests, but the refuge is mostly overgrown by low and dense shrubs of alder, willow, aspen, elder and paper birch, making the island almost impassable for everyone except the approx. 3,000 Kodiak bears. The refuge has seven major rivers and eleven large lakes as well as marshes and wetlands. On the mountain slopes above the brush line, alpine heaths and sedges hug the mountain peaks that are the haunt of some 400 mountain goats. The Sitka spruce forest is what might be called a subarctic rainforest, with mosses and lichens hanging from the branches. Thick hummocks of spongy mosses cover the damp forest floors, creating a fertile soil for yard-high fiddlehead ferns, cranberry vines and blueberry shrubs. Along the coast there are sea otters, harbor seals and Dall's porpoises all year. Gray whales pass by on migration in April and November. Cape Chiniak and Narrow Cape on the east coast are the best lookouts for whale watching.

The staple food of the Kodiak bear in the summer is salmon, which return in their millions to spawn. The migration continues all summer until mid-October.

The strongest earthquake ever measured on the North American continent (8.6 on the Richter scale) hit southern Alaska in 1964. Most of Kodiak Island sank 5 feet (1.5 m) and a giant 39-foot (12-m) wave wiped out half of downtown Kodiak—today one of the USA's largest fishing ports, with salmon, halibut and king crab as the major catch.

Fauna of interest

MAMMALS: Brown bear (Kodiak bear), river otter, stoat, mule deer, elk, mountain goat, American beaver, snowshoe hare, Steller's sea lion, northern fur seal, sea otter, harbor seal, Dall's porpoise, harbor porpoise, gray whale, fin whale, humpback whale, beluga, killer whale, Pacific white-sided dolphin.

BIRDS: Great northern diver, 3 species of

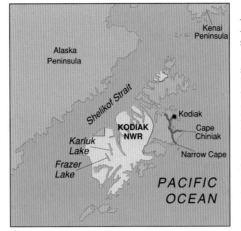

cormorants, emperor goose, 20 species of ducks (e.g., harlequin duck, Barrow's goldeneye, Steller's eider, surf scoter, king eider), bald eagle, golden eagle, merlin, peregrine falcon, 8 species of waders, 13 species of auks (e.g., tufted puffin, pigeon guillemot, marbled murrelet, ancient murrelet, crested auklet), northern hawk-owl. More than 200 different bird species have been observed.

Seasons

May be visited all year, but best in the summer. Climate is constantly chilly and rainy. Kodiak has a temperate coastal climate. Most rain falls on the eastern part of the island, where the annual precipitation reaches 76 inches (1.9 m). Kodiak bears are easiest to spot June to October, when the salmon are returning to the streams. April and November are best for gray whales. Bald eagles and sea otters all year, while December to May is optimal for emperor geese, king eiders and Steller's eiders.

How to get there

International flight to Anchorage, domestic to Kodiak or ferry from Homer or Seward, which gives opportunities to watch marine mammals and birds. Seasickness pills are recommended. There are less than 93 miles (150 km) of roads out of Kodiak, scenic but with a low chance of spotting bears. The refuge lacks roads, and the only way to get there is by sea plane (up to an hour's flying time, depending on destination) or by boat that can be chartered in Kodiak. A good place for bears is O'Malley River, between Karluk and Frazer Lake to the southwest. Up-to-date information at the visitors' center in Kodiak.

Accommodation/food/camping

There are hotels, eating-places and stores in Kodiak. In the refuge there are nine four-berth cabins for rent, six of which are located in good bear territory. Booking is necessary. You must be self-supporting, except for firewood (dead trees and branches on the ground). Camping and hiking permits can be obtained at the visitors' center.

Other areas

Katmai National Park, Alaska, USA, 6,371 square miles (16 500 sq km), was established in 1980 on Alaska Peninsula. Renowned for its 15 active volcanoes and for its salmon-fishing brown bears. There are approximately 750 bears in the park. The best place to view them is Brooks Falls, between Brooks Lake and Nanek Lake. Best time here is June until beginning of September. Several lodges and camping grounds. Book well in advance. Connected with Katmai is McNeil River State Sanctuary, housing up to 100 salmon-fishing bears in the white-water areas.

Denali National Park, Alaska, USA, 9,422 square miles (24 400 sq km), established in 1917. Magnificent alpine scenery, mainly above timber-line, with the highest peak in North America, Mount McKinley, at 20,318 feet (6193 m). Grizzly bear, gray wolf, moose, caribou, Dall's sheep, wolverine, lynx, American beaver, North American porcupine, golden eagle and gyrfalcon. Alaska's most popular national park, with 600,000 visitors annually. Best May to September. Shuttle bus along the 87-mile (140-km)-long gravel road. Hotels, camping grounds and hiking trails.

Pribiloff Islands, Alaska, USA, slightly more than 77 square miles (200 sq km), remotely located in the Bering Sea. The islands are a part of Alaska Maritime National Wildlife Refuge, and in the summer about 1 million northern fur seals congregate here to breed. Immense bird colonies, with 9 species of auks, red-faced cormorant, northern fulmar, red-legged kittiwake, black-legged kittiwake, harlequin duck. Best time is June to August, but, even then, cool, rainy and windy. One simple hotel.

Yukon Delta National Wildlife Refuge, Alaska, USA. A 4,247-square-mile (11 000-sq-km) windswept flat deltaland dotted with 50,000 lakes. One of North America's most important breeding grounds for wetland birds. Some 70 nesting species, e.g., a major share of the world's population of emperor geese, 3 other species of geese, tundra swans, spectacled eiders, sandhill cranes, 15 species of waders. Nunivak Island houses 500 muskoxen. Nearest city with hotels is Bethel. From here seaplanes and camping.

Kamtjatka, Russia, a peninsula extending more than 620 miles (1000 km) in the far east with magnificent wilderness and more than 100 volcanoes. Over 9,000 salmon-catching brown bears and numerous breeding Steller's sea-eagles. Bering Island has impressive auk colonies and huge rookeries of northern fur seals. Trips are arranged each year.

MAGNUS ELANDER

Sea Mammals in
Monterey Bay, California, USA

The Pacific Ocean rolls and thunders in to Point Pinos in Monterey Bay. Great waves smash onto the rocks and become white-foamed turmoil, filling the air with salt spray. A white, opalescent film blanks my sunglasses, windshield and camera lenses. Dimly I see flights of brown pelicans sweep in formation above the boiling waters, elegantly avoiding them. Just as a wave rises to engulf them, they are lifted over the top and into the following trough.

Small rafts of sea otters dive for food in the surf. These are often hard to distinguish from the harbor seals and young sea lions that frequent these waters, but one sea otter is lazily floating on its back, munching a fresh catch of crab, and there is no mistaking it.

Sea otters have their own ways of handling mussels, crabs, oysters and squid. They will dive for a rock to break open shellfish that resist their teeth. It seems an enviable life, floating on one's back, munching the freshest of *fruits de mer*, but every day, one must catch and eat 22 pounds (10 kg)—quite a lot for an animal that rarely weighs more than 66 pounds (30 kg).

As they are now a protected species, they have regained their former fearlessness toward humans and swim among the boats in Monterey harbor. Their favorite haunt is Coast Guard Wharf, where we get an intimate glimpse of their family life from a few yards away. They take no notice of spectators.

Winter is peak season for whale-watching, another major Monterey Bay attraction. Organized boat excursions bring you in close contact with the magnificent gray whale without getting your feet wet. Between ten thousand and twenty thousand whales pass Monterey Bay annually on their way from summer waters in the Bering Strait to their breeding grounds in the area off Baja California in Mexico.

Our visit is in summer. At dawn in early August, the mists of night still hang low over the chilly waters of the bay. A long, sandy beach leads us to Año Nuevo, along the coast, where we hear hollow, echoing snores, repeated with varying intensity and seemingly amplified by the banks of morning fog.

The sounds become more and more improbable and are accompanied by thunderous splashes. The elephant seals are holding their morning concert.

We approach their colony under cover of an embankment. As we peek over the edge, we see hundreds of elephant seals packed tightly together on the beach. Some have dragged themselves a hundred yards (100 m) from the water to rest under bushes. There won't be much shade for them later in the day, when the sun has burnt off the fog.

It seems an enviable life, floating on one's back, munching the freshest of fruits de mer, but for sea otters it is everyday life. Unlike whales and seals, the sea otter has no insulating layer of blubber. Instead it uses high metabolism and dense fur to retain body heat.

Magnus Elander

It is fur-shedding time, and the animals are far from beautiful. Their short-haired fur crackles and falls off in chunks. They throw sand over their backs with their flippers to speed up the process. A group of males who have not started to shed lie squabbling in the shallow water. Other males want to measure their strength, and suddenly small groups are attacking one aother, with much splashing and bellowing. Two- and three-ton mountains of male blubber clash and trumpet in ritual battle, slashing at each other's throats. It looks like a warmup for more serious fighting, which can rage until the sea is red with blood.

But this morning, they cool off. By midmorning the seals are sluggish, and there is relative peace in the colony. When we leave Año Nuevo, only the distant howling of a group of sea lions is heard above the surf. The next performance of the elephant seals will be at daybreak tomorrow.

Violent slashes at an opponent's neck decide the outcome of the elephant seals' mating battle in the shallows (opposite page). During fur-shedding time the animals fast on the beach for weeks (above). To save energy they hold their breath for up to 25 minutes at a time and look stone dead. The California sea lion (right) on the other hand is always active and regularly holds loud concerts.

Description

Monterey Bay is located some 75 miles (120 km) south of San Francisco. The bay attracts not only naturalists, but also anglers, surfers, divers and vacationers in general. The coastline between Santa Cruz to the north and the Monterey Peninsula to the south has a local population of slightly more than half a million, but is visited by millions of tourists annually. The lack of heavy industry keeps the water in the bay relatively unpolluted.

The sea floor in Monterey Bay forms a long submarine canyon reaching all the way to the shore. This canyon brings cold water, rich in nutrients, to the surface and forms the basis for the extraordinarily abundant marine wildlife in the bay.

The sea otter has become a great tourist attraction in Monterey. At "Sea Otter Center," open seven days a week, up-to-date tips on where to see the animals are given.

At the far end of the Coast Guard Wharf there is a congregation of sea lions most of the year. Like the sea otters, they normally pay no attention to inquisitive human spectators. The dividing line separating human and sea-lion territories is a fence, erected to protect both parties. A hole in the net is convenient for taking close-up pictures of the sea lions.

Whale-watching is another major attraction in Monterey. Guided boat trips offer good opportunities to get close to gray whales in winter. Somewhere between 10,000 and 20,000 whales migrate through the area on their way from their summer haunts in Bering Sea in the far north, to the breeding grounds at Baja California, in Mexico. On the whale-watching tours, other whales and dolphins are frequently seen. There are special trips for ocean-bird viewing and lots of pelagic birds are also seen on deep-sea-fishing trips.

In Pacific Grove there is a small stand of Monterey pines near Lighthouse Avenue in the backyard of Butterfly Grove Inn. Tens of thousands, possibly a hundred thousand, monarch butterflies winter here in the middle of a residential area. Outside Santa Cruz, at the northern end of Monterey Bay, there is another cove housing monarch butterflies. From a visitors' center, Monarch Trail takes spectators in to the secluded haunt of the butterflies in a eucalyptus grove.

At Año Nuevo, just north of Monterey Bay, is one of the finest wildlife sanctuaries for marine mammals in North America. Harbor seals are abundant and sea lions (both California and Steller sea lions) breed here. But the big attraction is the northern elephant seals. From being on the verge of extinction at the turn of the century, their numbers have increased rapidly again as a consequence of wise legal protection. Today an estimate says there are 100,000 animals of the northern species. The elephant seals prefer remote, inaccessible islands off the coast, and Año Nuevo is the only haul-out beach on the

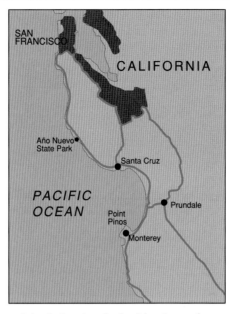

mainland where hundreds of the giant seals can be viewed at close distance.

Access to Año Nuevo State Reserve is only possible on guided hiking tours led by local scientists or students. Tours start from a visitors' center close to Highway 1.

Don't miss Monterey Bay Aquarium. It is not a zoo in the traditional sense, but a living museum that shows marine animals and submerged plant life in Monterey Bay.

Fauna of interest

MAMMALS: Northern elephant seal (sea elephant), California sea lion, Steller sea lion, harbor seal, gray whale, blue whale, dolphins (common dolphin and Pacific white-sided dolphin), killer whale, sea otter.

BIRDS: Black-footed albatross (summer), fulmar, spectacular numbers of shearwaters (sooty shearwater, short-tailed shearwater, flesh-footed shearwater), brown pelican, surf scoter and various auks (guillemot, pigeon guillemot, marbled murrelet, ancient murrelet, Cassin's auklet, rhinoceros auklet), several cormorants, several species of storm petrels, American black oystercatcher, black turnstone.

INSECTS: Monarch butterfly.

Seasons

Monterey Bay is often embedded in morning fogs formed as the cold water from the Pacific Ocean comes in contact with the warm air over land, but generally the weather is nice and stable, except for the winter months.

Elephant seals are seen all year. They haul out to give birth to their pups and mate in December to March (maximum numbers at the end of January). Molting is in April to August. In September to November juveniles come ashore to rest.

Sea otters, sea lions, dolphins and harbor seals may be seen all year.

The migration of the gray whale continues

from end of December throughout January. They turn north again in March/April. Monarch butterflies are viewed from beginning of October to March.

How to get there

International flight to San Francisco. By car along Highway 1—the coastal route, one of the most spectacular in the USA—a one-hour drive south to Año Nuevo. From the visitors' center guided tours start (several each day) to the elephant seals, a hike of 2.5 miles (4 km) round trip. Farther south along Highway 1, about 19 miles (30 km), is Santa Cruz and Natural Bridges State Beach, with monarch butterflies. From Fisherman's Wharf in Monterey, there are many boat tours for whale-watching, ocean-bird viewing or sport fishing. Book in advance during the peak season.

Accommodation/food/camping

No accommodation at Año Nuevo, and overnight camping is not permitted. Nearest is Santa Cruz, where, like in Monterey and Pacific Grove, a wide selection of hotels, motels, stores and eating-places for all budgets is available.

Other areas

Within reach by car from Monterey Bay are the renowned national parks *Yosemite* and *Sequioa*, with world-famous scenery and giant sequoia trees.

Mono Lake, California, USA, east of the Sierra Nevada range, on the border to Nevada, is less known but well worth a visit. Mono Lake is a very productive saline lake with myriads of nesting and staging birds. Few species but great numbers. 50,000 nesting California gulls, 100,000 Wilson's phalaropes and more than 20,000 red-necked phalaropes make a stop-over here in July/August; 700,000 eared grebe stage here in September. Accommodation and visitors' center in Lee Vining.

San Francisco Bay, California, USA, is a staging area for hundreds of thousands of waders and ducks (except May to July). The wetlands are surrounded by one of North America's most densely populated urban areas and have been reduced to a small fraction of their original size by land reclamation. But still this is one of North America's best wetland areas for wintering birds. Easy access, but smog is often dense from cars and aircraft.

Olympic National Park, Washington, USA, has a coastal fauna similar to that in Monterey. The national park, 1,386 square miles (3590 sq km), covers two separate areas; the western part is an extensive stretch of almost virgin Pacific Ocean coast. Best is Ozette Lake. Bald eagle, sea otter, river otter, whitetail deer, mule deer, elk, black bear, tufted puffin rookeries, gray whale, peregrine falcon.

FRANÇOIS GOHIER

Nursery of Gray Whales
Laguna San Ignacio, Baja California, Mexico

Whooooosh! The cloud of steam from the whale's blow hangs in the air for a few seconds. Everybody on board turns to see a 49-foot (15-m)-long, 30-ton gray whale surface a few yards away.

"It's a female!" someone yells. "She's got a calf with her!" This is confirmed by a miniature blow from the calf. It moves jerkily, like a baby taking its first steps. When the expelled steam dissolves in the warm summer air, mother and calf are lying side by side on the surface.

Their blowholes are wide open as they breathe in fresh air. They are curious and glide straight at our panga (an open Mexican fishing-boat). Before she hits the boat, the mother whale lifts her gigantic head and we see the 6.5-foot (2-m)-long arc of the corner of her mouth stretching back to an eye the size of a dinner plate.

Our gazes lock. She is confident in her natural environment. Last winter she mated, and maybe two months ago she calved here. During her gestation she swam 4,970 miles (8000 km) northwards along the west coast of North America to the rich waters of the Bering Sea, between Alaska and the Chukchi Peninsula of Russia.

She spent the summer feeding there to build up the thick layer of blubber needed to produce the very fat milk that is the calf's only food. In late autumn she swam back to Laguna San Ignacio to give birth. This is the longest known mammal migration. The calf weighed about 1 ton at birth and, in a month, when it leaves Baja California, it will have doubled its weight.

Our Mexican skipper calls "our" whales *las*

133

FRANCOIS GOHIER

amistosas, "the kind ones." Only one whale in ten dares approach so close to the boats. Research has not explained why. The approach occurs more often here, in Laguna San Ignacio, than anywhere else in Baja California.

When the calf lies alongside the gunwale, we all bend over and stretch out to pat it. We are trying to tell the whale that our intentions are honorable. Maybe we want to apologize for the intensive commercial whaling that almost wiped out the species twenty years ago. But the gray whale has recovered, and scientists reckon that there are almost 25,000 of them today, almost as many as before the slaughter.

The sun is setting over the Pacific, coloring the sky crimson, and the wind dies slowly. The whale and calf sink casually into the 82-foot (25-m)-deep waters of the lagoon. A couple of minutes later, they reappear quite a way off, this time in the company of half a dozen playful dolphins. Perhaps the calf makes them childish. They surf on the mother whale's bow wave, the way they do on the bow waves of big ships. Every time the

The gray whale is a coastal animal and is often seen close to the shore. It lives mainly on bottom-living crustaceans, and is not as specialized at eating plankton as are the other baleen whales.

calf surfaces to breathe, the dolphins go wild and jump high in the air.

The dolphins, of course, are whales themselves, although we don't usually think of them as such because they are (relatively) so small. In fact, they are quite large animals, up to 11 feet (3.3 m) long, and remarkably intelligent. Since ancient times, they have been known as the friends of sailors and used as heraldic figures and good luck charms.

We now see whales blowing everywhere. We count at least fifty, but there may be four hundred in the lagoon. Several thousand gray whales visit San Ignacio every year to mate or calve. Just as many whale-watchers come, too. From the human, and probably the whale, perspective, too, it is quite a spectacle.

Description

Baja California is a long, narrow and sparsely populated peninsula that stretches 808 miles (1300 km) from Tijuana in the north to Cabo San Lucas in the south. Since 1973 a road connects the north and the south. To the east of the peninsula lies the Mar de Cortéz, while the Pacific lies to the west. Baja California is desert and semi-desert with many different sorts of cacti. Fresh water is in short supply. A mountain range with almost 6,560-foot (2000-m) peaks runs along the eastern side of the peninsula. On the Pacific coast, which is flat with long beaches, there are three large lagoons where the gray whales gather in large pods either to calve or to mate. The lagoons are carefully protected by the Mexican authorities and only two are open for whale-watching.

Laguna San Ignacio is a shallow bay, 342 miles (550 km) from the southern tip of Baja California. It stretches 16 miles (25 km) into the dry landscape. Its greatest depth is 82 feet (25 m). A deep channel through the lagoon leads into the shallow area where the whales calve. No whale-watchers are allowed in here, only in the outer perimeters. The terrain here consists of sand dunes and low-lying desert, and there are no roads. The only way to get there is by sea or air. The lagoon is famous for the "friendliness" of many of its whales, which allow you to pat and stroke them. About 3,000 whale-watchers visit the area annually.

Laguna Ojo de Liébre, or Scammon Lagoon, lies a further 93 miles (150 km) northwards. No tourism is allowed here at the present time.

Bahía Magdalena, 124 miles (200 km) south of Laguna San Ignacio, can be reached by road from the city of La Paz. A number of low islands outside the bay protect the area from the Pacific Ocean. About 12,000 visitors come every season.

Fauna of interest

MAMMALS: Gray whale, California sea lion. On cruises around Baja California you can also see blue whale, Bryde's whale, sei whale, fin whale, minke whale, humpback whale, sperm whale, short-finned pilot whale, killer whale, dolphins (common dolphin, Pacific white-sided dolphin).

BIRDS: Great frigatebird, blue-footed booby, red-billed tropicbird, brown pelican.

Seasons

Gray whales can be seen from January to April. The end of February, when the females with their calves are on the way out toward deeper waters, passing those areas where tourists are allowed, is the best time. Some whales stay put until May/June, but anyone visiting then must be prepared for very hot weather.

Travel arrangements

International flight to San Diego in the USA or to Tijuana in Mexico. It is easiest then to

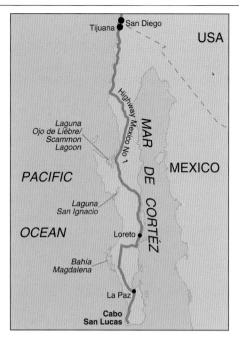

take an organized tour by boat or by chartered aircraft directly to Laguna San Ignacio. There are plenty of tour operators to choose from, offering trips that are usually 5–8 days long. Alternatively you can fly domestic to La Paz and continue by rented car or organized tour to Magdalena Bay. Boat charters can be booked with local fishermen.

Accommodation/food/lodging

No accommodation, food or camping are available in the area. Visitors must be self-sufficient or sign on for an organized tour.

Other areas

Sea cruises from La Paz to Loreto, Mar de Cortéz, Mexico. One of the richest waters in the world, with over 650 fish species. Excellent chances of seeing the blue whale, the world's largest living animal. Also chances to sight fin whale, Bryde's whale, minke whale, sperm whale, killer whale, short-finned pilot whale and gray whale. On islands in the Mar de Cortéz there are also colonies of California sea lion and birds such as great frigatebird, brown booby, blue-footed booby, brown pelican and red-billed tropicbird. Best from January to April.

Midriff Islands in the Mar de Cortéz, Mexico. A group of fifty islands about 248 miles (400 km) north of Loreto on the east coast of Baja California. Enormous quantities of fish, birds, dolphins and whales. Boat trips from Loreto.

Isla San Pedro Martir, breeding grounds for blue-footed booby, red-billed tropicbird and brown pelican. There are plenty of stationary fin whales and dolphins around the Isla Sal Si Puedes and Isla San Lorenzo. Everywhere is perfect for snorkeling.

Sea cruise from La Paz to Magdalena Bay, Mar de Cortéz and the Pacific Ocean, Mexico. Great numbers of whales and dolphins. In the Mar de Cortéz there are fin whale and minke whale. At the southern tip of Baja California there are plenty of humpback whale. Bottle-nosed dolphins and common dolphins are often seen in large pods and sometimes green sea turtle, hammerhead sharks, and even whale shark. Along the western coast of Baja there are good chances of seeing blue whale. Plenty of gray whale near the coast. Best from January to April.

The brown pelican is common around the coasts of Baja California, where it fishes by nosediving on its prey.

Bear Country
Jasper National Park, Alberta, Canada

A big black bear sits with her cub at the side of the road. As a cyclist approaches, she ambles into the middle of the road, with her cub following hesitantly.

The man on the bike is about to have the experience of a lifetime. He is leaning forward and pedaling furiously, oblivious to the bears. At the last moment he sees them and brakes until the bike almost stands on its front wheel.

The bear is unbothered, for this is bear country. She eyes the terrified cyclist and moves over to a ditch, where she finds her second cub lying dead. She pushes it with her snout, but it does not move. It has been hit by a car, for this scenic land of the Utopia Mountains is automobile country, too. She moves off into the forest with her surviving cub.

Near Maligne Lake, we see a solitary cow moose anxiously swiveling her head from side to side. A large wolf is stalking her, moving in ever-tighter circles.

The grizzly has a reputation for being a fierce bear, said to be quite different from the more placid black bear or the European brown bear. But the truth is that most bears are very peaceful. And all bears can be very dangerous.

It gets its name from its grizzled fur, but the grisly stories told about encounters with grizzlies have made it the villain of the Rockies.

Black bears in the wild are mainly vegetarians, but they will eat almost anything. Since civilization has brought garbage dumps to the wilderness, some bears have turned their attention to garbage.

The round-faced hump-backed grizzlies are more carnivorous. They used to range from Mexico to Alaska but are now found mostly in national parks or deep in the northern wilds.

Like other bears, they have poor hearing and eyesight but an excellent sense of smell. They are born blind, toothless and about the size of rats, so they have to be sheltered in the mother's den until they are big enough to accompany her outside.

After that, they are no longer helpless, and about to grow very powerful.

Two grizzly bears in a beautiful meadow start their day with a ferocious wrestling match. A third grizzly joins in, and passing motorists halt to watch. When a fourth bear joins the fray, a busload of Japanese tourists stops.

One tourist insists on having his wife in the picture while he snaps the bear fight, but a park ranger intervenes and sees to it that everyone stays in their vehicles. Eventually the bears tire of the attention and disappear into the virgin wilderness.

Suddenly it attacks, striking at the moose's rear legs, while she lashes out with her front hooves. In the end, she escapes by rushing into nearby rapids, where she stands up to her belly in the glacial water. The wolf tries to follow but is swept out of his depth. He patrols the riverbank all evening, while the moose stands stock-still in the river. Neither will give in. When night falls they are still there. We don't know what happens, but they are both gone by morning.

Around Maligne Lake, the biggest lake in Jasper National Park, mule deer (above) and grizzly bears (right) are often seen.

TORBJORN ARVIDSON

TORBJORN ARVIDSON

The black bear (left) comes in a variety of shades, from jet black to light brown. The grizzly (above) is always brown and has a characteristically broad, round face, while the black bear's is slimmer and more doglike. You can always tell the grizzly by its powerful shoulders and humped back.

Description

Jasper National Park was founded in 1907 and is the largest Canadian national park in the Rockies. It lies on the eastern slope of the Continental Divide watershed and is part of a group of national parks (Jasper, Banff, Yoho and Kootenay) that make up the UN-designated Rocky Mountains World Heritage Site. Jasper is the richest in wildlife and covers 4,170 square miles (10 800 sq km) of wide valleys, high mountains, glaciers, forests, mountain tundra and unregulated rivers. In the southern section of the park, the Columbia Icefield glacier has the greatest concentration of peaks over 9,843 feet (3000 m) in the whole of the Rocky Mountains.

Tongues of ice from its most famous glacier, the Athabasca Glacier on the border between Jasper and Banff, spread far down along the surrounding valleys. The most dramatically beautiful mountain in the park is the pyramid-shaped Mt. Edith Cavell, southwest of the city of Jasper.

There are more than 745 miles (1200 km) of hiking trails in the park, providing many opportunities for one-day or multiday hikes. There are two major roads through the park, Icefield Parkway running north–south from the southern entrance to the city of Jasper, and Highway 16 running east–west through the city. There are also several very beautiful roads up in the mountains. The largest lake is Maligne Lake, 3 1/2 miles (22 km) long and 318 feet (97 m) deep, which is fed with water from the glaciers in the south.

While it is possible to hike and camp in the park, it is easier and safer to travel through the area by car. Pure wilderness starts only a few meters away from the car door. A fine hike with splendid scenery starts in the parking lot at the north side of Mt. Edith Cavell and goes up via the Angel Glacier to the treeless mountain tundra. The best chance of seeing bears and other big game animals is along Icefield Parkway, Highway 16 or Maligne Lake Road in the early morning or late evening.

The largest population of protected bear is found here, with 150–200 grizzly bears and about 300 black bears. Black bears can also be seen in and around the city of Jasper. There are also several thousand elk, while moose, white-tailed deer and caribou are common. There are plenty of bighorn sheep and mountain goat high up on the mountainsides and on the mountain tundra, which are only accessible on foot. However, you have a good chance of seeing these animals from the car at Tangle Ridge near Columbia Icefield, and at Disaster Point on the eastern branch of Highway 16. The park has a thriving wolf population with a number of separate packs. The best chance of hearing wolves howl is along the North and South Boundary hiking trails.

Fauna of interest

MAMMALS: Grizzly bear, black bear, mountain lion, wolf, coyote, bighorn sheep, mountain goat, caribou, elk, moose, white-tailed deer,

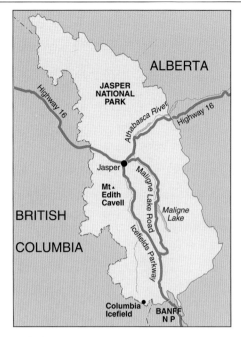

mule deer, porcupine, hoary marmot, beaver, snow-shoe hare, pika.

BIRDS: Bald eagle, golden eagle, Canada goose, great horned owl, blue grouse, spruce grouse, common loon, Clark's nutcracker.

Seasons

The park is open all year round. In peak season, July and August, it can be crowded on the roads and in the hotels and campsites. It is easiest to see bears, caribou, and moose during the off-season (May/June and September/October). Black bears are best seen in the early summer (May/June) as they eat dandelions by the roadside, and in the summer when the berries in the valleys have ripened. Both grizzly and black bears hibernate from the end of October to early May. Bighorn sheep and mountain goat are more accessible in the winter when

they come down from the high mountain slopes. Elk can also be seen in the winter.

How to get there

International flight to Edmonton or Calgary. Train or bus to the city of Jasper, where you can rent a car. Current information on hiking trails, camping permits, maps etc. are available all year round in the park's visitors' center in Jasper.

Accommodation/food/lodging

There is plenty of accommodation available, from 400-room hotels to simple campsites. For the car-borne there are 10 campsites with space for over 1,700 tents or camper-vans. The biggest camp sites (*Whistlers* and *Wapiti*) have all mod cons and are south of the city of Jasper. Most sites are open from mid-May to mid-October.

Other areas

Banff National Park, Alberta, Canada. Founded in 1885, it is the oldest, most popular and probably the most scenic of Canada's national parks. Covering 2,500 square miles (6641 sq km), it is rich in grizzly and black bear, caribou, moose, bighorn sheep, mountain goat and wolf. Best in April/May and September/October.

Yoho National Park, British Columbia, Canada. 507 square miles (1313 sq km) just north of Kootenay and bordering on Banff in the east. Spectacular, with 30 peaks over 9,843 feet (3000 m). Mainly the same fauna as Jasper, with moose, elk, wolf, coyote but fewer bears. Perfect for backpacking, with 250-mile (400-km) trails into every corner of the park.

Kootenay National Park, British Columbia, Canada. 541 square miles (1402 sq km) just west of Banff with mainly the same fauna as Jasper but better wilderness hiking and camping.

Despite its speed, the least chipmunk (here at Moraine Bluff in Banff National Park) often ends up as food for predators such as coyotes and bears. There are more grizzlies than black bears in Banff.

STAFFAN WIDSTRAND

Caribou Tundra
Ivvavik National Park, Yukon Territory, Canada

The pilot lands his Twin Otter on bumpy mountain tundra in an Arctic wilderness. This has been described as the Serengeti of the North because of the richness of its wildlife. We shall see.

Hundreds of pounds of expedition gear are unloaded, and two large rubber rafts made ready. Somehow we get everything packed in the rafts and float off downstream under the midnight sun. Occasionally we pass by a bald or a golden eagle on the lookout from the top of a spruce tree. All is still, apart from the gentle rushing of the Firth River.

Next morning we find fresh grizzly tracks on the riverbank below our tent.

The river narrows as the landscape is crisscrossed by thousand-year-old caribou migration trails—curving parallel lines that decorate the mountainsides in regular patterns. Rounding a bend in the river, we find a mag-

nificent, full-grown wolf gazing at us from the bank. It does not move until the rafts are very close, then it turns and disappears. Hiking the next day, we meet four other wolves, three gray and one white, who suddenly appear in front of us on the caribou trail. Later, we almost fall into an occupied wolf's den.

At the park rangers' center in Sheep Creek, Chief Ranger Vicki Sahangtien gives us the disheartening news that we have missed the caribou migration across the river by a few days.

"It took more than five days for the 100,000-head herd to cross the river. It was an incredible sight. The whole landscape seemed to be on the move." Nature is fickle and unforeseeable.

We set up camp at Engistiaq, a hill that rises in isolated majesty over the open tundra. This is an ancient hunters' settlement, and one of the most important archeological sites in arctic North America, with finds dating back 8,000 years. Bones of mammoth, mastodon, *Artio-*

dactylus horse, caribou and muskox have been unearthed here, along with tools of their hunters. From the hilltop, our local guide, James Pokiak, spots thirteen muskoxen, five golden eagles and five grizzly bears. We ourselves see some Arctic squirrels that live in holes in the ground.

"Grizzly snacks," says James.

For the last few miles on our journey toward the sea, we have to drag, push and paddle the rafts through the shallow delta water. Sometimes we scare up a muskox from the banks. Or does he scare us? When we reach the edge of the Arctic Ocean, big yellow-billed loons pass by in full summer plumage, while flocks of surf scoters bob up and down among the offshore ice floes.

On the flight back to Inuvik, we finally sight the caribou. Thousand upon thousand of them surge over the tundra below us. The pilot is able to land briefly on an esker nearby, and soon the animals are milling around us. Over the low rumble of their hooves comes the clicking of tens of thousands of foot joints.

The great caribou migration has taken place each season for thousands of years. They calve in May or June and continue on the move a few weeks later.

Migration is their way of life, as it is for migratory birds, but there the comparison ends. It takes far longer for a great brown mass of heavy animals to surge across the landscape, and it makes an even more dramatic sight. We are glad we first saw it from the air.

The caribou of the tundra and the Barren Lands are big deer with large lateral hooves and hairy muzzles. They are reindeer, a variety of the Scandinavian reindeer depicted on Christmas cards.

Laplanders have succeeded in domesticating some of their reindeer, and have introduced them to Arctic Canada and Alaska. They feed on lichens, including "reindeer moss," which somehow manages to sustain them on their incredible journeys.

The "Serengeti of the Arctic" is fickle, but the wildlife is certainly there.

There is much wildlife to be seen where the Firth River meanders across the open tundra in Ivvavik National Park: caribou, Dall sheep, muskox, moose, wolf and grizzly bear. This is primordial nature, but it lies in a region with huge oil reserves, which may endanger its future as a national park. The region is sometimes called "Kuwait on ice." Caribou (left) in full autumn colors make their way toward their forest winter quarters.

141

The numbers of caribou have increased dramatically almost throughout North America in the past twenty years. The Porcupine River herd in Ivvavik is reckoned to hold 200,000 head. The size of a herd has always fluctuated heavily due to natural causes—unsuitable snow conditions can kill off half the herd during a single winter. The peregrine falcon (below) thrives in the parts of the Canadian tundra where there is plenty of prey. The most popular items on its menu are ducks, gulls and larger waders.

142

Description

The early stretches of the Firth River flow quietly northwards through a broad valley sparsely covered with trees in the 480-million-year-old British Mountains. In the later stages it throws itself with enormous power down through a long, narrow canyon, and then out into the open arctic tundra, slowing down as it finally reaches the Arctic Ocean. The river is the artery of the relatively recently established Ivvavik National Park, which was created through an agreement with the Inuvialuit Eskimos in 1984. Ivvavik National Park is a part of a vast, untouched and mainly protected wildlife area. In the west it joins up with the continually controversial Arctic National Wildlife Refuge (ANWR) in Alaska, and in the south it joins up with Vuntut National Park, making in total a protected region of over 17,376 square miles (45 000 sq km)! Ivvavik is sometimes called a "Serengeti of the Arctic" and more than 200,000 caribou migrate here for summer grazing and calving. Very few people live here, and the only human activities are some hunting, fishing and tourism. In 1995 the total number of visitors to Ivvavik National Park was not more than two hundred…

However, there are enormous amounts of oil and gas under the tundra and the coastal stretches of the Beaufort Sea, and many powerful forces want to exploit this. The same situation has also arisen in the Alaskan side of the ANWR. There is talk of a "Kuwait on ice," but the last word has not yet been said. The Inuvialuit Eskimos have had the right of veto since the agreement in 1984 and so far they have used it to stop all drilling for oil under the sea, as there is so far no technology available to deal with oil spills under the ice. A spill under the ice would destroy the Inuvialuits' traditional beluga-whale hunting, which they have hitherto valued more than millions of dollars in royalties from oil.

One of the Inuvialuits' traditional hunting grounds is Herschel Island, a small island just off the Firth River estuary, where they mainly hunt beluga whale, seal and polar bear.

At the end of the 19th century it was also a central port for American whalers hunting bowhead whales. Up to 1,500 whale hunters would live here during the summers. Today, Herschel Island is protected as a Territorial Park, with rich birdlife as well as muskox, caribou and grizzly bear.

Fauna of interest

BIRDS: Gyrfalcon, peregrine falcon, golden eagle, bald eagle, rough-legged buzzard, gray plover, snowy owl, long-tailed jaeger, pomarine jaeger, yellow-billed loon, whistling swan, harlequin duck, sandhill crane, Canada goose.

MAMMALS: Grizzly, polar bear (only in winter), red fox, Arctic fox, wolf, wolverine, lynx, Dall sheep, Arctic ground squirrel, muskox, caribou (about 200,000), beluga whale (along the entire coast).

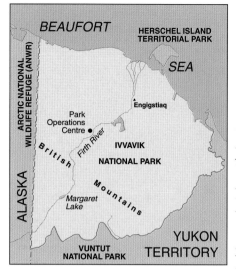

Seasons

May be visited all year round, but only by special permit from Inuvik and under local guidance. Caribou calve in May/June and migrate across the coastal plain and the north slopes of the British Mountains normally in June and the first two weeks of July. This is also high season for the thousands of beluga whales that pass by. (They can often be seen from Herschel Island itself.) June/July are the best birding months. In August/September the caribou are on the move toward Old Crow Flats and Vuntut National Park. Sometimes thousands of them can be seen along the Dempster Highway.

How to get there

International flight to Calgary, Edmonton or Yellowknife, domestic flights from there to Inuvik. You can also drive along the famous Dempster Highway, which ends in Inuvik. From Inuvik charter a boat along the coast or charter a light aircraft. Many Canadian nature-tour operators, and even local companies, arrange expeditions for smaller groups, with hiking, river trips and/or a visit to Herschel Island. Sightseeing by air with stop-offs on Herschel Island are arranged daily from Inuvik during the summer, as well as visits to Tuktuyaktuk. Permission is needed to visit Ivvavik National Park. Tour operators in Inuvik can arrange that and other logistics.

Accommodation/food/lodging

No eating places or hotels of any kind in the park. This is pure wilderness. Bring your own camping gear.

Other areas

Arctic National Wildlife Refuge, Alaska, USA. Same terrain and fauna as Ivvavik but just across the Alaskan border. Reach it via Prudhoe Bay and/or Kaktovik. Many American tour operators arrange expeditions.

Vuntut National Park, Yukon Territory, Canada. New national park, created by a land claims settlement with the Gwich'in Indians. Vast swamplands, tundra and pine forests. Part of the autumn and winter grounds for the caribou herds that calve in Ivvavik and ANWR. Reach it via Inuvik. Local guides and permits obligatory.

Kobuk River National Park, Alaska, USA. 1,776 square miles (4600 sq km) national park, on land between the taiga and the tundra. Black bear, moose, 600,000 caribou, grizzly, wolf, lynx. The caribou are best seen from end-August to early September. In August comes the great salmon migration, with excellent fishing and a lot of grizzly bear on the Squirrel River, northwards from Kiana. Reach it via Kotzebue and Kiana or Ambler. Travel by canoe, kayak, raft or motorboat. Onion Portage at Ambler is an archeological site where finds indicate continual settlement for over 10,000 years.

Tuktut–Nogait National Park, NWT, Canada. New national park with almost the same terrain and fauna as Ivvavik, but in a less hilly landscape. Reach it via Paulatuk and Inuvik. Local guides and permits obligatory.

The Arctic ground squirrel is a rodent which exists in huge numbers along the mainland coast at the tundra. They live underground in huge colonies and provide the staple diet for predators and raptors. The grizzly bear is particularly fond of them and likes to spend full summer days digging up their nests.

STAFFAN WIDSTRAND

The Polar Bear Capital of the World
Cape Churchill National Park, Manitoba, Canada

Two young polar bears are sparring out on the ice, like boys in a school-yard, jabbing, punching, feinting, ducking and wrestling, while twenty older bears lie around, ignoring them. The youngsters are testing their strength in preparation for the battles of adult life. Snow powder whirls about in the counterlight and the combatants look both strong and dangerous. Which they are. In fact, the only real danger a polar bear faces is another, stronger bear or an armed human.

Of all the land beasts of prey, the polar bear is the biggest and the most powerful. Anything that lives in its environment, man included, is a possible quarry. That's why we watch the young bears' exhibition bout from the safety of our tundra buggy.

One of our group drops his bonnet and it falls on the ice. The bears pounce on it and play with the bonnet almost without a break for two hours. They look like cuddly, giant dogs. Then a bigger bear approaches and peers through the tundra buggy's window. We feel a kinship with the goldfish when the cat looks into its bowl ...

Our guide keeps a loaded pump-action shotgun behind the driver's seat. Four thousand tourists take these bear-watching trips each year and only one has been injured—badly bitten in the arm when he hung it out the buggy window for too long. Nowadays no chances are taken with these potentially very dangerous animals.

The bears appear indifferent to the attention, although four big tundra transports have gathered close by them. They rest and wait until the ice has formed on the sea and they can venture out on it. They take eco-tourism as it comes and seem completely undisturbed by it. One after the other, they approach the buggy and sniff it. Sometimes one of them takes a nibble at a wheel. Perhaps they see us as a welcome diversion in their otherwise uniform seal-hunting lives?

A big one sits under an observation ramp at the rear of our vehicle and sticks its long, soft nose through a small hole in the ramp floor. Foolishly, I touch the big, wet nose, which is immediately withdrawn. Again it comes up through the hole and I pat it gently. Twice more and, as I stretch out my hand again, the bear's paw strikes like lightning through the hole. It misses my hand, but the claws leave deep scores in the plywood floor.

Churchill never aspired to be the polar bear capital of Canada, but the tiny tundra town just happened to be built right in the middle of an ancient migration route for the polar bears. They pass by here on the way from their summering grounds to the pack ice on Hudson Bay.

The polar bear is the largest land carnivore, an animal that sees everything that moves as a possible dinner. And that includes man! Churchill is the best place to safely see polar bears at close hand.

From the "tundra buggy" the bears can be studied at arm's length!

The great white beasts are fascinating to tourists, but downright scary when they wander into town.

Bears found within town limits are sedated and brought to a "Polar Bear Jail," from which they are later released by truck or helicopter, out on the ice.

They're great to watch, but would you want to have them around the house?

A gyrfalcon races past and scares up a snow squall of winter-white willow ptarmigan. On the tundra we see a few caribou and Arctic fox. An ivory gull flies overhead. Soon Hudson Bay will be iced over, and all the polar bears will leave Churchill for the season.

As soon as the sea has frozen, the polar bears return to the ice, where they can find their favorite food, the fat seals. The bears must eat a lot of seal blubber every autumn in order to build up a good layer of fat to protect them against the bitter cold of winter.

Sometimes, a polar bear is "adopted" by a little Arctic fox (left), which then follows it at a safe distance. The fox knows that there is always food to be found in the bear's tracks, either leftovers from its meals or even its droppings.

Staffan Widstrand

Description

The town of Churchill, "The Polar Bear Capital of the World," is situated in northern Manitoba, where the Churchill River runs into Hudson Bay. Churchill is the most easily accessible spot for viewing polar bear in the entire Arctic region. The bears can be seen at close hand and in large numbers. Ten to twenty bears in the one day is not unusual. Churchill is unique because it is the only place in the world where you can see polar bears on the streets. During October and November of 1994, two hundred bears were captured in the town! They were then transported far out onto the Hudson Bay ice. No hunting is permitted in the area, so the bears here are not as shy as they are in other areas.

Outside the town is the recently established Cape Churchill National Park, which has one of the world's largest concentrations of polar bear dens. As many as three hundred bears give birth here every winter, right in the middle of the severest cold. During the spring the bears fatten themselves on seals they catch out on the ice, and when the ice melts in July they are forced to come ashore. At the end of October, when the bears regather at the coast, most of them have eaten virtually nothing since July, but have been surviving on their reserves of fat.

Despite Churchill's relatively southerly position 497 miles (800 km) south of the Polar Circle, the landscape and the climate are Arctic. This is where the border runs between the taiga and the open tundra. The country is flat, with no dominant features. There are only a few wind-twisted trees to be found around the town of Churchill.

The area lies in the Northern Light belt, and during the darker part of the year the Aurora Borealis is often seen, a captivating and impressive display across the night skies.

Fauna of interest

BIRDS:
Winter: Gyrfalcon, willow ptarmigan, rock ptarmigan, ivory gull, glaucous gull, raven, gray jay, hawk owl, snowy owl, snow bunting.
Summer: Ross's gull, Pacific loon, rough-legged buzzard, peregrine falcon, long-tailed jaeger, lesser snow goose, Canada goose, waders.

MAMMALS: Polar bear, caribou, Arctic fox, Arctic hare, bearded seal, ringed seal, beluga whale, wolf, red fox, wolverine, lynx, moose, river otter, beaver.

Seasons

The polar bear season is short. It is best from about October 25 to November 15; the later it is the more bears you can see, the more snow has fallen and the colder it gets. Which also means the greater the risk that the sea will freeze and the bears will be gone for the season. The beluga whale season is best during June and July but continues into August. As many as 3,000 beluga whales gather in the relatively

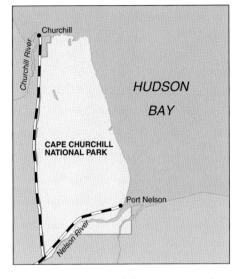

clear water of the Churchill estuary to slough their skins, feed, calve and mate. Seal spotting is best from March to June, when the seals lie on the ice sunbathing.

From the beginning of June to mid-July is the best time for watching the rich tundra birdlife. The Northern Lights are best seen between October and April. The sea normally freezes over in mid-November and does not break up until June.

How to get there

International flight to Winnipeg, and from there by domestic flight (4 hours) or by train (38 hours). From most North American cities, Churchill is the most accessible and rewarding Arctic destination. The last week of October and the first week of November are usually fully booked well in advance.

Local companies arrange day excursions to the tundra during the summer and the polar bear season in so-called tundra buggies, huge train-like vehicles with enormous wheels to avoid damage to the tundra. These are one-day tours with competent guides. Special photo safaris in smaller vehicles are available.

You can also rent a car yourself and explore the huge network of roads on your own. Then you won't see so many polar bears, but you will have a greater chance of seeing wolves and other taiga species. Daily boat trips depart in July/August to see seals and beluga whales at close hand. Bird-watching trips to the tundra are also arranged during the summer.

Accommodation/food/lodging

Several hotels, wilderness lodges and bed & breakfast establishments, both in the town and outside it. You can also overnight among the polar bears in *Tundra Buggy Lodge*—a simple mobile hotel. There are restaurants and bars in Churchill. If you stay at a bed & breakfast you can often cook for yourself. Plenty of well-stocked shops with food, and even a good assortment of Arctic clothing.

Other areas

Aulavik National Park, Banks Island, NWT, Canada. 80,000 muskox (1996), almost half of the world population, live here on the wide open spaces of the tundra. Also caribou, Arctic hare, Arctic fox, Arctic wolf, polar bear, as well as a typical High Arctic bird population, with species like king eider, long-tailed jaeger, snowy owl, American golden plover, gray plover, and rock ptarmigan. Fairly inaccessible, but can be reached via Resolute or Inuvik to Sachs Harbour.

Bathurst Inlet, Nunavut, Canada. Huge bay and low-lying wet tundra with high-Arctic wildlife. For instance, hundreds of thousands of caribou pass through the area during spring and autumn. Also muskox, grizzly bear, gyrfalcon, peregrine falcon and a number of other typical tundra species. Lodging at *Bathurst Inlet Lodge*, where guides and trips can be arranged.

Cunningham Inlet, Somerset Island, Nunavut, Canada. Summering site for thousands of beluga whales in July/August. The whales can be seen at close hand in the clear Arctic water. Occasional polar bears, seals of several species and High Arctic birdlife. Several companies arrange trips. Over-nighting, Inuit guides, full board and transport from Resolute. On the flight from Resolute narwhal can be sighted in the Barrow Strait.

The people of Churchill call their town "The Polar Bear Capital of the World." It is one of the few towns in the world where polar bears walk the streets. If the bears come into town, they are captured and released way out on the sea ice.

STAFFAN WIDSTRAND

Whale-Watching around the World

It begins like a scene from a horror movie. A diver swims in the crystal-clear waters of a fjord. Suddenly the 3-foot (1-m)-high dorsal fin of a killer whale comes up out of the water behind him. Twenty-three feet (7 m) long and 5 tons in weight, the flesh-eater races at the defenseless man. The man in the water reacts unexpectedly. When the whale has passed him at arm's length, he gestures triumphantly. "It looked at me. It had a herring in the corner of its mouth, just a yard away!"

He is a whale researcher, following one of the most efficient predators in the oceans. It eats everything, from herrings to blue whales—but never people.

Some forty killer-whale dorsal fins stick out of the water near the shore in Stefjord, Norway. The pale-pink light of an arctic November, and the snow-clad mountains dropping steeply into the depths of the fjord, make a magnificent setting for these beautifully streamlined whales.

For several winters Tysfjord, southwest of Narvik in northern Norway, has seen the world's biggest concentration of coast-hugging killer whales. Nowhere else can you see so many so close, and against such a spectacular background. Not everyone is happy about this. Enormous shoals of herring gather in these fjords and the whales eat them in vast quantities. Commercial fishermen, who claim the herring as theirs, want to bring back hunting of killer whales.

The killer whale, or *orca*, is an extra-large dolphin, with all the dolphin's intelligence. You can teach it tricks and get it to perform in aquatic shows, where it has proven to be a very loveable crature.

It will hunt almost anything, either on its own, or in packs. They are known to have attacked and killed huge whales, although their principal victims are seals, porpoises, fish and seabirds. One had the remains of 13 porpoises and 14 seals in its stomach.

Now for a change of scene: Icy Strait, off Juneau in Alaska, is one of North America's best-known whale

149

regions, particularly in July. A mile ahead of our boat, a humpback can be seen blowing, and Captain Howard Robinson steers slowly toward it. Again and again the whale blows moisture-laden air from its lungs in a cloud of waterdrops which can be seen several miles off. When the whale-safari boat is about 160 feet (50 m) away, the humpback dives slowly and with great dignity. A blackish-gray back arches in the water, an elegantly shaped fluke turns indolently up in the air, and 40 tons of whale disappears into the depths.

Another blow is sighted farther ahead, and then another. Two more of the twenty humpbacks summering in the area are making their presence known. This time the whale-watchers are so close to a 43-foot (13-m) whopper that its blow spatters the foredeck. It is level with the bow when it finally dives.

After an hour among the humpbacks, what everyone has been waiting and hoping for happens. A heavy whale shoots out of the water like a torpedo, bends backwards and falls back with a colossal splash. Jubilation breaks out on deck—expressed in six languages—and in response the whale does it again, then again and again.

Humpback whales in Alaska. They may rear out of the water to impress the female whales, but they certainly impress the onlookers … On a calm day a whale blow can be seen from several miles away (above). Each individual whale has its own shape and color of fluke (below). Researchers photograph them and are able to identify hundreds of individual humpbacks, which are then monitored, year after year.

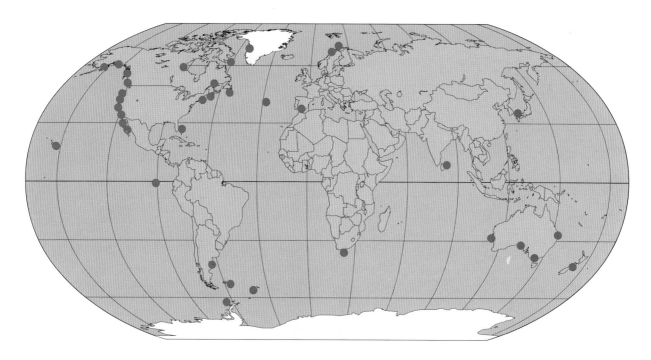

WHALE-WATCHING AROUND THE WORLD

Whale-watching has become a multimillion-dollar industry. In 1991, four million eco-tourists spent some $350 million (US) on whale safaris around the world. These figures are approaching the income from the now-abandoned commercial whaling. Might the whales even be more profitable alive than slaughtered?

• *Andenes, Andøya*, Norway: Sperm whale, killer whale, minke whale. May to September. Daily cruises.

• *Tysfjord*, Norway: Some hundred killer whales. Mid-October to mid-February. Cruises operated from Storjord.

• *Gibraltar*, United Kingdom/Spain: Dolphins and porpoises by the thousands, mainly April to November. Seen from the Cádiz–Tangier ferries or on special cruises from Shepherd Marina, Gibraltar.

• *Disko Bay*, West Greenland: Humpback whale, bowhead whale, minke whale, sperm whale, sei whale, fin whale, killer whale. Summer months. Whales are frequently seen from the coast liners *Kununguak* and *Disko* between Narsarssuak and Upernavik.

• *The Azores*, Portugal: Sperm whale. Boat trips from Lajes du Pico on the island of Pico.

• *Stellwagen Bank/Cape Cod*, Massachusetts, USA: Humpback whale, dolphins, fin whale, minke whale, northern right whale, porpoises, Atlantic white-sided dolphin. April to October. Large whale-watching industry. Whales seen on all cruises. May be viewed from the shore at Race Point. Embarking ports Provincetown, Plymouth, Boston, Barnstable, Gloucester, Portsmouth, Rye.

• *Grand Manan Island*, Bay of Fundy, New Brunswick, Canada: Northern right whale (calving area), humpback whale, minke whale, fin whale, dolphins, porpoises. August to beginning of October.

• *Southeastern Newfoundland*, Canada: Humpback whale, fin whale, minke whale, long-finned pilot whale, dolphins. Sometimes called "the Serengeti of whales." May to October. Whales may be seen from several places on the shore. Many tour boats at Trinity and St. John's.

• *St. Lawrence River*, Quebec, Canada: Beluga, blue whale, fin whale, minke whale, dolphins. June to October. Best June to August. Boat trips from ports like Baie Ste. Catherine, Tadoussac, Rivière du Loup, Les Escoumins and Sept-Iles. Whales may be spotted from land at several places.

• *Lancaster Sound*, NWT, Canada: Hundreds of belugas, narwhals. July/August.

• *Churchill River*, Hudson Bay, Manitoba, Canada: 3,000 belugas in July/August. Cruises are arranged.

• *California and Oregon coasts*, USA: A total of 20,000 gray whales pass on migration. Peak season January/February and March/April.

Can be spotted from almost any elevated coastal cliff. Whale cruises from most major ports.

• *Farallon Islands*, California, USA: Blue whale, humpback whale, minke whale, killer whale, dolphins, porpoises, pelagic birds. May to October, especially June to September. Gray whales from mid-December to March. Cruises depart from Monterey and San Francisco.

• *Vancouver Island/Queen Charlotte Islands*, B.C., Canada: Killer whale (June to September), gray whale (June to September and March to April), minke whale, porpoises. Cruising ports are Vancouver, Sointula, Port McNeil, Campbell River, Telegraph Cove, Alert Bay, Tofino and Ucluelet. Several tour operators.

• *San Juan Islands/Johnstone Strait*, Washington, USA: Killer whale June to September. Gray whale October to December and March to May. Seen from viewing points on land or boat cruises. Cruises depart from Friday Harbor, Westport and Seattle.

• *Monterey*, California, USA: Humpback whale and blue whale July to September. Gray whale best in January. Several species of dolphins and porpoises all year. Daily cruises in season.

• *Baffin Island*, NWT, Canada: Beluga, narwhal, bowhead whale. May/June. Multiday trips only.

• *Alaska*, USA: Eight whale-watching ports: Kodiak, Seward, Whittier, Gustavus, Juneau, Sitka, Petersburg, and Wrangell. Day trips and longer cruises. Whales may also be seen from the coast liners. Prince William's Sound, Icy Strait, Glacier Bay and Frederick Sound are all relatively accessible whale-watching areas. 300 humpback whales, hundreds of gray whales, porpoises, minke whales, fin whales, killer whales. May to September, best June to August. Gray whales in November/December and April/May.

• *Lahaina/Maalea Harbor*, Maui, Hawaii, USA: Calving grounds for 1,200 humpback whales December to April. Best seen in February/March. Dolphins, false killer whales and short-finned pilot whales all year. Whales may be spotted from the upper floors of the luxurious beach hotels. A wide selection of cruises to choose from.

• *West End & Hope Town*, Elbow Cay, Grand Bahama, USA: Spotted dolphins to pat and swim with. Season is April to October. Boat cruises are organized.

• *Puerto Pirámides*, Valdés Peninsula, Chubut, Argentina: Southern right whales calve here July to November. Killer whales hunt sea-lion pups on the beaches at Punta Norte January to April. In addition, dolphins. Whale-watching trips from Puerto Pirámides.

• *Galápagos Islands*, Ecuador: Dolphins, sperm whales (north of Isabela Island), minke whales, fin whales. Season January to April. Whales are mainly spotted on designated whale-watching tours. Dolphins are seen by most visitors.

• *Lagunas San Ignacio/Ojo de Liébre/Guerrero Negro/Magdalena*, Baja California, Mexico: Hundreds of calving gray whales. Season from mid-December to March, best in January/February.

• *Islas Revillagegido*, Baja California, Mexico: Calving grounds for an impressive number of humpback whales. Season is March. Also dolphins.

• *Bahia de Banderas/Puerto Ballarta, Mar de Cortéz*, Baja California, Mexico: One of the world's top places for whale-watching. Blue whales (20), humpback whales, fin whales, Bryde's whales, killer whales, dolphins, minke whales, short-finned pilot whales, sperm whales. Puerto Ballarta, Loreto och La Paz for boat cruises. Also multiday trips. January to April, best March/April.

• *Trincomalee*, Sri Lanka: Sperm whales, dolphins and blue whales. Cruises are organized frequently. Whales may also be spotted from land, at Swami Rock.

• *Toyo Kochi*, Shikoku, Japan: Sperm whales, sei whales, Bryde's whales, dolphins, killer whales. Season March to October.

• *Kaikoura*, South Island, New Zealand: Sperm whales (all year), swimming with dolphins, humpback whales (June/July). Boat cruises daily from the marina in Kaikoura.

• *Monkey Mia, Shark Bay*, Perth, Australia: Swimming with dolphins all year round.

• *Hervey Bay*, Fraser Island, Queensland, Australia: Humpback whales. Season August to October.

• *Warrnambol*, Victoria, Australia: Calving grounds for southern right whales. Season May to October. Lookouts on land.

• *Victor Harbour*, Adelaide, Australia: Southern right whales at close range between June and October.

• *Cape Town–Port Elisabeth*, South Africa: Southern right whales and dolphins. May to November, best in September. Hermanus at Walker Bay and the cliffs at Robberg, Plettenberg Bay are excellent lookouts.

• *Antarctica/South Georgia/Falkland Islands:* A traditional commercial whaling area, nowadays protected. Blue whales, humpback whales, sei whales, fin whales, southern right whales, minke whales, killer whales, sperm whales, dolphins. Multiweek cruises. Season November to March.

A minke whale in Antartica. Minkes are the most numerous of baleen whales. A couple of whaling nations want to hunt them commercially again.

STEFAN LUNDGREN

Coral Reefs around the World

A strip of yellow-white beach etches the boundary between the deep green tropical vegetation and the intense turquoise-blue of the sea. The island, a few miles in circumference, is the top of a coral reef. Similar islands dot the horizon. Lighter shades of blue water indicate reefs that do not quite reach the surface. The sun gets even hotter, and cotton-wool clouds glide by.

With a Northerner's suspicion, my youngest son tests the water with his big toe. A shout of joy signals at least 77°F (25°C), and the whole family plunges into waist-deep water. With snorkels and masks, a whole new world opens up beneath us.

Fish, sea cucumbers, sea anemones, polyps and clams, all an arm's length away; shapes and colors blended as in a kaleidoscope. Blue-green parrot fish, bright-red and blue-spotted coral polyps, a shoal of square, flat, yellow butterfly fish. Even harlequin fish, with red, white and blue stripes.

Grunts from my elder son's snorkel shatter my underwater bliss. He points to a giant clam, half-embedded in the coral, with the wavy edges of its shell hanging ominously half-open. We approach very cautiously and it suddenly snaps shut. We sense the tremendous force behind the snap.

This is the killer clam. Get your hand or foot snapped in it and you'll never get free. Divers have been held under until they drowned. A couple of rainbow-colored parrot fish interrupt my reflections on this ghastly fate. In the still water you can hear them crunching away at the limestone shell of the coral to get

there is no drama. The sharks ignore us and pass by a few yards away, slowly moving their tails.

Nearly an hour has gone by since we left the boat. Our air supply is running out and it is time to go back up. The boat has been following our air bubbles, and when we surface it is only a few yards away.

We are content to return to our own environment, but we'd go back down again anytime.

We had stared the killer of the deep straight in the eyes, and returned to tell the tale. The truth is, of course, that reef sharks are not considered to be very dangerous.

Plenty of other divers have done the same; daredevils play with sharks the way others "tame" lions, but, once again, you never know. ...

Most species are quite harmless, but swimmers do sometimes get maimed or eaten by the fearsome great white shark and others.

Only in recent decades has the magic of the blue water reefs been opened up to us through the invention of snorkels and scuba gear—a gigantic part of our world that we had never been able to explore before.

Okay, there are sharks down there. And killer clams and poisonous reef creatures. Highway traffic is also risky, yet most people still drive cars. The underwater wonder is absolutely worth the slight risk.

at the living polyp inside. These big fish are unafraid and make you feel welcome in this mysterious environment.

The diving-school boat bobs in long, heavy waves between two islands. Two of us do a back somersault, leaving the Indian Ocean rollers above and sinking slowly into the depths. Our air bubbles rise in a small cloud. It is a fantastic feeling to be suspended 65 feet (20 m) down, weightlessly moving in the clear water. Visibility is more than 165 feet (50 m) and soon we can vaguely see the edge of the reef. The strength of the current is noticeable now, and we have to hold on to some solid coral so as not to drift away.

Then our eyes register unmistakable shapes in the distance. Two reef sharks! They swim lazily in our direction. Our pulses race. For a few tense moments the sharks swim menacingly closer. Statistics show that nearly all encounters between sharks and humans end undramatically, but you never know. Sharks are the most feared of fish. Tremble! they seem to say. But

On the Red Sea, off the Sudanese coast, you can get really close to a gray reef shark (above left). Most encounters with sharks are not dangerous, even if nerve-jangling. Coral reefs are the haunt of many thousands of species of fish, such as the red hawk fish (below) from the reefs around Kuredu in the Maldives.

155

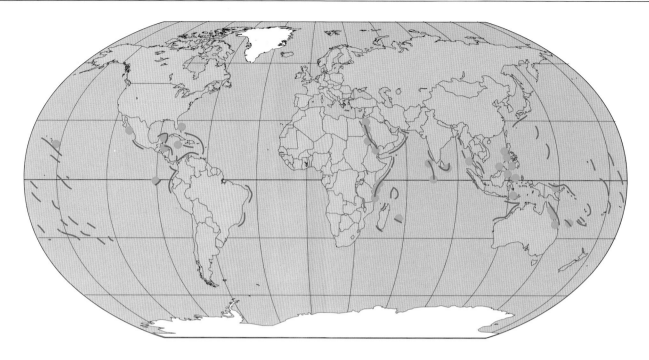

A SELECTION OF CORAL REEFS AROUND THE WORLD

Coral reefs occur in relatively shallow waters in a wide belt around the Equator, always more extensive and more numerous in species to the east of the continents. From Florida, surrounding many islands in the Caribbean Sea and onwards to southern Brazil. From the Red Sea along the Arabian Peninsula and to the east coast of Africa, all the way down to Mozambique, including Madagascar. All of Southeast Asia, the east coast of Australia and around many islands in the Indian Ocean and the tropical parts of the Pacific Ocean.

It is not necessary to have a diver's certificate to enjoy the coral reefs, since there are many ways to encounter submarine wildlife: cruising in a glass-bottomed boat, floating on the surface peeping through a glass-fronted mask, skin-diving with a snorkel, or more advanced scuba-diving. It is only a matter of selecting a place to suit your gear and experience. Most of the time a glass-fronted mask, flippers and snorkel are enough.

Corals are built up by millions of tiny animals, anthozoa, no larger than a fingernail. Every little anthozoa forms a tiny limestone cup from excreta, which becomes their housing, and colonies with countless anthozoa successively, and inch by inch, build up giant coral reefs. As the old generations die off, their lime skeletons remain, on top of which new generations continue to build. The Great Barrier Reef off the east coast of Australia is the largest structure that living organisms have accomplished. It extends for 1,305 miles (2100 km) and covers an area comparable to the size of the United Kingdom.

With their innumerable cavities, nooks and crevices, the coral reefs provide a living environment for a world of life that triggers every imagination, from sea anemones and thousands of different brightly colored fish of all shapes, to immense giant clams, groupers, leatherback turtles, rays, skates and sharks. The coral reefs are among the richest habitats in the world in terms of diversity of species, second only to the tropical rainforests.

Descriptions

• *Elat*, Israel: Suitable for beginners at snorkeling and diving. Season all year but most comfortable in the spring. Summer is very hot.

• *Sharm el Sheikh/Naama Bay, and Ra's Muhammad Nature Reserve*, Sinai peninsula, Egypt: Regarded as one of the best coral reefs for diving in world. Hammerhead shark, whitetip reef shark, rays and skates, manta ray, sea turtles, moray eels, shoals of barracuda, and large grouper (up to 8 feet/2.5 m), bumphead wrasse. Season all year around, but best in August/September. Suitable for advanced scuba-diving, since the coral reef descends abruptly to a depth of 2,297 feet (700 m). Other good diving places are Straits of Tirana, Dunraven, Ras Umm Sid, Tower och Ras Nasrani.

• *Hurghada*, Egypt: Good diving and snorkeling but not comparable to Ra's Muhammad. Several diving centers.

• *Shab Rumis*, Sudan: Renowned shark location immediately north of Port Sudan. Scuba-diving only. Best access to diving locations along the coast of Sudan is by chartered boats from Port Sudan.

• *Farasan Islands*, Yemen: Advanced diving. Access by chartered boats. Archipelago with magnificent coral reefs.

• *Great and Little Basses Reef*, Sri Lanka: The best diving places in Sri Lanka, with groupers, sharks, tunny-fish, barracudas and porpoises. Located off Ruhuna/Yala National Park in the southeast. Best from March to mid-April. Access via Hambantota. Sandstone reefs, advanced diving.

• *Wasini and Kisite-Mpunguti Marine Reserve*, Kenya: Excellent for snorkeling. Access via Shimoni.

• *Malindi-Watamu Marine National Parks*, Kenya: Easily accessible. Glass-bottomed boats, snorkeling, diving centers at most of the major beach hotels in Watamu.

• *Zanzibar*, Tanzania: Several diving centers, excellent snorkeling, particularly southwest of the main island. There are also very good reefs at Pemba and Mafia Island.

• *Mauritius*: Good diving at Whale Rock, Merville, Cathedral, Flic-en-Flac, Round Island and Roche Zozo. Several diving centers.

• *Maldive Islands* with some 1,200 islands in 19 tiny atolls. About 60 islands have diving centers and diving locations, but Kanifinolhu, Meerufenfushi and Kuredu are the best. Good all year round, but peak season is November to April. Rainy and changeable weather in the summer. Best season for manta ray is October/November.

• *Chagos Archipelago*, Chagos Bank (belongs to the United Kingdom): Atoll archipelago south of the Maldive Islands. More sharks than other fish!

• *Similan and Koh Surin*, Phuket, Thailand: Boat tours departing from Phuket.

Best time is November to March. Monsoon rains May to October. Suitable for inexperienced. The reefs around Phuket are somewhat worn down.

• *Semporna Islands*, Sabah, Malaysia: Reefs as excellent as at Sipadan.

• *Sipadan Island Marine Park*, Sabah, Malaysia: The visible peak of a submerged mountain descending sharply some 1,969 feet (600 m) on all sides. Magnificent and easily accessible coral reefs housing, among others, sea turtles and hammerhead sharks. Visibility to 230 feet (70 m). According to Jacques Cousteau, one of the super reefs of the world.

• *Selingan Turtle Island*, Sabah, Malaysia: Excellent scuba-diving and snorkeling with sea turtles, etc. Access via Sandakan.

• *Apo Reef, Mindoro Strait*, Philippines: Spectacular scuba-diving and snorkeling, best February to May. Is reached via San José, Mindoro.

• *Basterra Reef and Tubbataha Reef Marine National Park*, Philippines: In the middle of Sulu Sea, and is reached via Puerto Princesa, Palawan. March to June.

• *Moal Boal and Badian Island*, Cebu, Philippines: Still very unexploited. Charter boats.

• *Sumilon Island*, Philippines: Off the southeastern coast of Cebu. Is reached via Dumaguete, Negros. All year.

• *El Nido, Bacuit archipelago*, Palawan, Philippines: Is reached via Liminancong. November to June.

• *Bunaken Marine Park and Arakan Marine Area*, Manado Bay, Sulawesi, Indonesia: Snorkeling and scuba-diving all year with, for instance, whale sharks and dugongs. Diving centers and guides.

• *Tukang Besi Islands*, Indonesia: Southeast of Sulawesi in the Banda Sea.

• *Bismarck archipelago*, Papua New Guinea. Unexploited. A few diving centers exist, for instance, at Emma Reef and Christine Reef, Walindi. Regarded as some of the best reefs for diving in the world. April to November.

• *Great Barrier Reef Marine Park*, Australia: Comprises 2,500 separate coral reefs and islands. An extraordinarily diverse habitat with 2,000 species of fish and 200 different types of corals. Cairns is a suitable and easily accessible starting point. Boat cruises to various destinations from most ports along the coast, including Port Douglas, Townsville and Gladstone. Best April to December.

• *Green Island National Park and Michelmas Cay*, off Cairns, is suitable for in-experienced. One or multiday trips by boat farther out in the Barrier Reef are best for advanced scuba-diving.

• *Heron Island National Park*, with boat or helicopter service from Gladstone, 44 miles (70 km) away, is the most accessible reef in the outer Barrier Reef. Large numbers of different sea turtles haul out for egg laying October to April, hatching December to May. Hotel, no camping. Extremely popular. Scuba-diving and snorkeling.

• *Lizard Island*. No coral island in itself, but surrounded by excellent and easily accessible coral reefs. Snorkeling and scuba-diving near the shore all around the island. Vicinity to the outer Barrier Reef including Cod Hole, with up to 6.5-foot (2-m) groupers (potato cod) and large moray eels. Big game fishing (black marlin) September to December. Expensive and luxurious. Air service from Cairns.

• *Orpheus Island*. Rocky island surrounded by coral reefs close to the shore. Excellent snorkeling and scuba-diving with, for instance, sea turtles, dolphins and sting-rays. Luxurious hotel. Boat service or seaplanes. Day trips departing from Townsville.

• *North West Island National Park*, the largest single reef in the Great Barrier Reef with, among others, sea turtles. Day trips by boat from Rosslyn Bay or by helicopter. Camping.

• *The Coral Sea* between the Great Barrier Reef, Australia, and New Caledonia, France: Coral atolls reaching the surface. Extremely clear water with myriads of different species. Another of the top diving areas in the world.

• *Molokini Islet*, Maui, Hawaii, USA: A partly submerged volcano crater 3 miles (5 km) south of Maui, with coral reefs inside the crater. Sharks, manta rays and, from December to May, also humpback whales. Snorkeling as well as scuba-diving. Daily boat trips departing from several ports on Maui. Other good diving locations are Honoloa Bay and La Perouse Bay Marine Preserves.

• *Cocos Islands*, Costa Rica: Off the west coast of Costa Rica in the Pacific Ocean. For experienced divers. Several species of sharks, e.g., hammerheads. Boat cruises with accommodation on board depart from Costa Rica.

• *Galápagos Islands*, Ecuador: Boat charter for scuba-diving, while snorkeling is possible on all island trips. Whitetip and blacktip reef sharks, hammerhead sharks, manta rays and sea turtles.

• *Virgin Islands National Park*, USA: The main island, St. John, is surrounded by easily accessible coral reefs. A sign-posted submarine trail at Trunk Bay. Good snorkeling. Hotel and camping. Snorkeling also at the neighboring island St. Croix.

• *Isla de Cozumel*, Mexico: December to April. Suitable for beginners. Access via Cancun.

• *Lighthouse Reef Reserve*, Belize: The fifth-largest barrier reef in the world with barracudas, groupers, spider crabs and angelfish. Swimming with dolphins. Best December to April. Hotels.

• *Key Biscayne National Underwater Park*, Florida, USA: Comprising 282 square miles (730 sq km), with only 4 percent (45 tiny coral islands) above the surface. 200 species of fish, sea turtles and manatees. Day trips by boat, glass-bottomed boats, snorkeling and scuba-diving.

• *Mar de Cortéz*, Baja California, Mexico. Diving trips depart from the southern tip. Hammerhead sharks, manta rays.

Butterfly fish near the island of Kuredu in the Maldives.

Afterword

You might imagine eco-touring your dream destination to be difficult and/or expensive. Yet, most of the places we describe can be visited simply by putting together an airline ticket, map, bus ticket and/or the hire of a car. For those who want to journey independently, there are detailed guidebooks, accounts by earlier travelers, and masses of information. For those wanting something more convenient, various specialized tour operators offer a great variety of tours to practically anywhere in the world. Believe us, it's not particularly difficult! What's more, your visit may contribute directly to nature conservation.

In many places, we've seen how well-organized eco-touring can support both conservation and economic development. In many countries, eco-tourism is the *only* significant force for conservation. It is a means of protecting natural environments, since these can acquire greater economic value if left undisturbed for eco-tourists than exploited and destroyed.

All eco-tourism is based on certain fundamental principles, which we believe all travelers should be mindful of:

• Never contribute to the destruction of the natural resources you have come to experience. As a traveler, you have a responsibility. Try to travel in such a way as to contribute to and strengthen conservation. Patronize travel agencies which show the greatest regard for the environment. Leave behind nothing except footprints; take nothing except photos.

• Do not promote the extinction of rare animals, birds or plants by ill-advised souvenir buying. Do not buy such items as lion's claws, tortoise or turtle shells, ivory, crocodile skins, molluscs, live reptiles, orchids and corals.

• In the long run all conservation of primordial nature depends on whether the people living in the region want it preserved. Can your journey benefit the local population in some way? Can you hire their servants—as guides, porters, cooks? Can you buy local products?

• Check your travel agent's environmental awareness. Is the accommodation adapted to environmental demands? Does he work with eco-tourism? Is any part of the travel costs contributed to nature conservation? In what way will the trip benefit those who live in the area?

We've written this book because we ourselves have often needed one. We hope that you'll find it useful.

Safe journey!

Magnus Elander,   Staffan Widstrand

Magnus Elander   Staffan Widstrand

Acknowledgments

A brief word of thanks to all those who have made this book possible: cooks, fellow travelers, porters, boatmen, photographers, writers, mahouts, guides, dogteam owners, people who hired out kayaks, tour operators and conservationists.

Our very special thanks to the NATURBILD agency and its skilled, well-traveled photographers for the loan of the pictures we ourselves did not succeed in taking.

Thanks are also due to all those who offered advice, who shared with us their experience and knowledge gained in every corner of the earth, and were a sounding board for our ideas:

Per Alström, Tomas Bergenfeldt, Peter Bergman, Olle Carlsson, Hans Drake, Mats Forsberg, Johan Fredlund, Anders Haglund, Ragnar Hall, Peter Hanneberg, Per Jiborn, Kicki Lind, Stefan Lundgren, Hélène Lundgren, Rolf Magnusson, Olle Melander, Magnus Melin, Krister Mildh, Håkan Nunstedt, Jan Pedersen, Stefan Qvinth, Lotta Savegren, Stig Söderlind and Jan Wigsten.

We also wish to thank the photographers Torbjörn Arvidson, John Cancalosi, Ove Eriksson, Mats Forsberg, Christer Fredriksson, Anders Geidemark, Francois Gohier, Anders Haglund, Sven Halling, Bengt Hedberg, Kicki Lind, Stefan Lundgren, Magnus Melin, Håkan Nunstedt, Jan Pedersen, Stefan Qvinth and Hasse Schröder.

Pictures from the book are available from
NATURBILD
PICTURE AGENCY

Selected reading

Africa

Atkins, Chris and McIntyre, Simon. *Guide to Namibia and Botswana*. Chalfont St. Peter: Bradt Publications, 1991.

Bannister, Anthony and Johnson, Peter. *Okavango: Sea of Land, Land of Water*. New York: St. Martin's Press, 1997.

Bradt, Hilary. *Guide to Madagascar*. Chalfont St. Peter: Bradt Publications, 1994.

Crowther, Geoff and Finlay, Hugh. *East Africa—A Travel Survival Kit*. Hawthorne, Victoria: Lonely Planet Books, 1987.

Iwago, Mitsuaki. *Serengeti*. London: Thames & Hudson, 1987.

Norton, Boyd. *The Mountain Gorilla*. Stillwater, MN: Voyageur Press, 1990.

Orenstein, Ronald. *Elephants: Last of a Noble Line*. Toronto: Key Porter, 1997.

Owens, Delia and Owens, Mark. *Cry of the Kalahari*. New York: Houghton Mifflin, 1984.

Scott, Jonathan. *The Great Migration*. Emmaus, PA: Rodale Press, 1989.

North America

——. *National Geographic's Guide to the National Parks of the United States*. Washington, DC: National Geographic Society, 1992.

Grove, Noel. *Wild Lands for Wildlife: America's National Refuges*. Donald J. Crump, Ed. Washington, DC: National Geographic Society, 1984.

Harbury, Martin and Watts, Ron. *The Last of the Wild Horses*. Toronto: Key Porter, 1995.

Johnsgard, Paul A. *Ducks in the Wild: Conserving Waterfowl and Their Habitats*. Toronto: Key Porter, 1992.

Jones, John Oliver. *Where the Birds Are—A Guide to All 50 States and Canada*. New York: William Morrow, 1990.

Kraulis, J.A. *From Acadia to Yellowstone: The National Parks of the United States*. Toronto: Key Porter, 1996.

Kraulis, J.A. *Rocky Mountains*. Toronto: Key Porter, 1994.

Lawrence, R.D. *Trail of the Wolf*. Toronto: Key Porter, 1993.

Mason, Bill. *Song of the Paddle: An Illustrated Guide to Wilderness Camping*. Toronto: Key Porter, 1994.

McNamee, Kevin. *National Parks of Canada*. Toronto: Key Porter, 1994.

Melham, Tom. *Alaska's Wildlife Treasures*. Washington, DC: National Geographic Society, 1994.

Obee, Bruce. *Wolf: Wild Hunter of North America*. Toronto: Key Porter, 1994.

Pettingill, Olin S. Jr. *A Guide to Bird Finding—East of the Mississippi*. New York: Oxford University Press, 1981.

Pettingill, Olin S. Jr. *A Guide to Bird Finding—West of the Mississippi*. New York: Oxford University Press, 1981.

Raffin, James, Ed. *Wild Waters: Canoeing North America's Wilderness Rivers*. Toronto: Key Porter, 1997.

Russell, Andy. *Great Bear Adventures: True Tales from the Wild*. Toronto: Key Porter, 1994.

Russell, Charles. *Spirit Bear: Encounters with the White Bear of the Western Rainforest*. Toronto: Key Porter, 1995.

Schmidt, Jeremy. *Adventuring in the Rockies*. Toronto: Key Porter, 1994.

South and Central America

——. *Amazon Wildlife (Insight Guides Series)*. Boston: Houghton Mifflin, 1993.

Bernhardson, Wayne and Samagalski, Alan. *Chile & Easter Island—A Travel Survival Kit*. Berkeley: Lonely Planet Books, 1993.

Bradt, Hilary and Schepens, Petra. *Backpacking and Trekking in Peru and Bolivia*. Chalfont St. Peter: Bradt Publications, 1980.

Emmons, Louise and Feer, Francois. *Neotropical Rainforest Mammals—A Field Guide*. Chicago: University of Chicago Press, 1990.

Gentry, Alwyn H., Ed. *Four Neotropical Rainforests*. New Haven: Yale University Press, 1991.

Murphy, William L. *A Birder's Guide to Trinidad and Tobago*. Parkersburg, WV: Peregrine, 1995.

Samagalski, Alan. *Argentina—A Travel Survival Kit*. Hawthorne, Victoria: Lonely Planet Books, 1989.

Australia

Chapman, John. *Bushwalking in Australia*. Hawthorne, Victoria: Lonely Planet Books, 1992.

Asia

——. *Indian Wildlife (Insight Guides Series)*. Boston: Houghton Mifflin, 1993.

Armington, Stan. *Trekking in the Nepal Himalayas*. Berkeley: Lonely Planet Books, 1994.

Antarctica

Moss, Sanford. *The Natural History of the Antarctic Peninsula*. New York: Columbia University Press, 1991.

General

——. *Animal Kingdoms: Wildlife Sanctuaries of the World*. Washington, DC: National Geographic Society, 1995.

Grace, Eric S. *Whale: Giant of the Ocean*. Toronto: Key Porter, 1996.

Mackay, Barry Kent. *The Birdwatcher's Companion*. Toronto: Key Porter, 1994.

Snyderman, Marty. *Shark: Endangered Predator of the Sea*. Toronto: Key Porter, 1995.

Williams, Heathcote. *Whale Nation*. London: Jonathan Cape, 1988.